Happy Hour at Home

LIBATIONS AND SMALL PLATES FOR EASY GET-TOGETHERS

BY BARBARA SCOTT-GOODMAN

RUNNING PRESS
PHILADELPHIA · LONDON

Books published by Running Press are available at special discounts for bulk purchases in the United States by corporations, institutions, and other organizations. For more information, please contact the Special Markets Department at the Perseus Books Group, 2300 Chestnut Street, Suite 200, Philadelphia, PA 19103, or call (800) 810-4145, ext. 5000, or e-mail special.markets@perseusbooks.com.

ISBN 978-0-7624-4585-1

Library of Congress Control Number: 2012942525
E-book ISBN 978-0-7624-4877-7

9   8   7   6   5   4   3   2   1
Digit on the right indicates the number of this printing

Cover and interior design by Barbara Scott-Goodman
Edited by Kristen Green Wiewora
Photography: Rita Maas
Food Stylist: Adrienne Anderson
Prop Stylist: Mariellen Melker
Typography: Bodoni and Franklin Gothic

Running Press Book Publishers
2300 Chestnut Street
Philadelphia, PA 19103-4371

Visit us on the web!
www.runningpresscooks.com

A toast to all of my dear friends and family
who helped me create this book!

Cheers!

table of contents

introduction

"Let's meet for a drink" is a welcome phrase that I often hear from friends who want to get together for an informal and sometimes impromptu evening. For obvious reasons, I always like to pick a spot that serves food at the bar in case that drink becomes a few more and the evening turns into a long, convivial night. Happily, many bars, from trendy city hotspots to sleepy small-town taverns, have re-vamped happy hour food and evolved from serving mundane snacks like salty nuts, popcorn, and chicken wings. Their kitchens are sending out delicious and innovative dishes such as pulled pork sliders, crispy fried vegetables, and mini crab cake sandwiches for their hungry customers to savor while sipping cocktails. In fact, recently some of my most memorable meals have not come from dining at high-end restaurants or stylish bistros, but from eating at the bar.

In these busy times, what's better than taking time to slow down and enjoy a well-made drink and a good bite to eat? Whether you stop by your favorite local watering hole for an after-work cocktail, glass of wine, or beer, or meet friends at a posh new spot—a snack, a nosh, a bite of something delicious is always welcome. So why not bring the happy hour home and enjoy a warm and relaxed evening? For a truly good time, get your friends together, and serve a few rounds of cocktails with some easy and elegant hors d'oeuvres.

There was a time when people thought the only thing to have with a dry martini was a cigarette, but dishes like Sherry-Braised Chorizo Bites (page 62) or Deviled Eggs with Smoked Trout and Watercress (page 19) are much better accompaniments. Pulled Pork Sliders (page 34) or mini meatballs (page 60) pair deliciously with a Sazerac (page 38), the classic New Orleans cocktail. And a Negroni (page 67) goes down very easily with a bite of Taleggio & Swiss Chard Crostini (page 53) or slice of homemade pizza topped with mozzarella, roasted tomatoes, and pancetta (page 56).

This book is a collection of recipes for snacks and small plates from all over the world that the at-home host can create to serve with cocktails. They include classic and innovative American bar fare, European bites and tapas, Asian plates, spicy Latin dishes, and inventive and refreshing tastes from the Caribbean islands. There are also a number of recipes for cocktails that pair well with these happy hour dishes, and which are sure to appeal to beginner bartenders as well as experienced mixologists.

This is not high-end, labor-intensive dinner party fare. This is straightforward food that is fun to make, eat, and enjoy with your family and friends. Whether you serve a few things to nibble on with cocktails before dinner, or choose to extend the happy hour and make a full-fledged meal with a variety of dishes, this food is sure to please cook and guests alike.

So, enjoy cooking, eating, and drinking with *Happy Hour at Home.* It's 5 o'clock somewhere.

CHAPTER 1

::::::::::::

cocktail extras

herb & vermouth-infused olives

THESE SAVORY OLIVES ARE A WONDERFUL ALTERNATIVE TO THE KIND YOU GET FROM A JAR. I LIKE TO SERVE THEM as part of a cheese and salumi plate, and they are a perfect garnish for martinis. Look for good-quality, large green olives when making these.

Makes 2 to 3 cups

8 ounces large green olives, such as Picholine, Cerignola, or Manzanilla

1 tablespoon kosher salt

1 tablespoon mixed whole peppercorns

Pinch of red pepper flakes

4 garlic cloves, peeled and halved

2 sprigs fresh rosemary

2 sprigs fresh thyme

1 small piece lemon peel

1 cup dry vermouth

¼ cup olive oil

Rinse and drain the olives, and set aside.

Combine 1 cup of water with the salt, peppercorns, red pepper flakes, garlic, rosemary, thyme, and lemon peel in a saucepan, and bring to a boil, stirring so the salt dissolves. Remove from the heat. Add the vermouth and olive oil, and let cool to room temperature, stirring occasionally.

Stir in the olives, and transfer to a clean glass container with a tight-fitting lid. Cover, and refrigerate for at least 6 hours or overnight before using. The olives will keep in the refrigerator for up to 2 weeks. Bring to room temperature before serving.

pickled cocktail onions

THESE PICKLED ONIONS ARE A CINCH TO MAKE, AND THEY ARE A FABULOUS GARNISH TO A GIBSON (PAGE 36) or an Aquavit Bloody Mary (page 69). They also are an excellent addition to a relish tray or vegetable platter.

Makes about 2 cups

1½ cups (about 10 ounces) small white pearl onions

2 cups dry vermouth

1 cup white vinegar

½ cup granulated sugar

1 tablespoon kosher salt

1 teaspoon mixed whole peppercorns

6 whole cloves

Bring a large pot of water to a boil. Add the onions, and cook for 3 minutes. Drain in a colander, and rinse with cold water. Cut the root ends off of the onions, and gently squeeze the opposite end until they pop out of their skins.

Put the vermouth, vinegar, sugar, salt, peppercorns, cloves and ½ cup water in a 2-quart saucepan, and bring to a boil, stirring constantly until the sugar and salt dissolve. Add the onions, and cook for 2 minutes. Remove from the heat.

Transfer the onions and brine into a clean glass container with a lid. Let cool to room temperature. Refrigerate for at least 6 hours before using. The onions will keep for up to 1 month in the refrigerator.

marinated fresh cherries

TAKE ADVANTAGE OF FRESH CHERRIES WHEN THEY'RE IN SEASON, AND MAKE A FEW JARS OF MARINATED CHERRIES for garnishing drinks. They also taste great over ice cream or frozen yogurt.

Makes 1 quart or 2 pints

⅔ cup granulated sugar

½ cup pomegranate juice

2 cups (about 1 pound) pitted fresh cherries

2 tablespoons fresh lemon juice

2 cinnamon sticks

1 teaspoon almond extract

Combine 1½ cups water with the sugar and pomegranate juice in a saucepan. Bring to a simmer over medium-high heat, stirring constantly, until the sugar dissolves. Add the cherries, lemon juice, cinnamon sticks, and almond extract, and simmer for 10 minutes. Remove from the heat, and let the cherries steep for 1 hour.

With a slotted spoon, remove the cherries to a lidded glass container. Strain the juice, and pour over the cherries to cover. Let cool to room temperature, then store in the refrigerator for at least 6 hours before using. The cherries will keep in the refrigerator for up to 2 weeks.

simple syrup

SIMPLE SYRUP IS A MIXTURE OF SUGAR AND WATER, AND IT IS AN IMPORTANT ADDITION TO ALL MANNER OF DRINKS. It's easy to prepare and is always good to have on hand in the refrigerator, since it keeps well. I prefer using 2 parts water to 1 part sugar (medium simple syrup), for most cocktails, which is the recipe I've given here.

Makes about 2 cups

1 cup granulated sugar

Combine the sugar with 2 cups of water in a heavy-bottomed saucepan, and bring to a gentle boil over medium-high heat, stirring to dissolve the sugar. Reduce the heat, and simmer until the sugar is completely dissolved and the syrup is slightly thickened, about 3 minutes.

Remove from the heat, and let cool to room temperature. Transfer to a clean container with a tight-fitting lid, cover, and refrigerate until ready to use. It will keep in the refrigerator for up to a month.

Variations:

Thin Simple Syrup: 3 parts water to 1 part sugar

Thick Simple Syrup: 1 part water to 1 part sugar

Herbed Syrup (left), Simple Syrup, (right), page 13

ginger syrup

SIMPLE SYRUP (PAGE 13) THAT IS INFUSED WITH FRESH GINGER IS AN EXCELLENT ADDITION TO ICED TEA AND lemonade, and it blends beautifully with bourbon and whiskey.

Makes about 1 cup

1 cup granulated sugar

4 (1-inch) pieces fresh ginger, trimmed and peeled

Combine ½ cup water with the sugar and ginger in a small saucepan, and stir. Bring to a boil over medium heat. Reduce the heat, and simmer, stirring occasionally, until the sugar is completely dissolved and the syrup is slightly thickened. Let cool, and strain into a clean container with a lid. Cover, and refrigerate until ready to use. The syrup will keep in the refrigerator, for up to 2 weeks.

herbed syrup

HERE'S A GOOD RECIPE TO MAKE IN THE SUMMER WHEN FRESH HERBS SUCH AS MINT, BASIL, AND LEMON verbena are available. Use a combination of herbs to make a very flavorful blend.

Makes about 1 cup

1 cup sugar

1 cup chopped fresh herbs like mint, basil, pineapple sage, and lemon verbena

Combine ½ cup water with the sugar and herbs in a small saucepan, and stir. Bring to a boil over medium heat. Reduce the heat, and simmer, stirring occasionally, until the sugar is completely dissolved and the syrup is slightly thickened. Let cool, and strain into a clean container with a lid. Cover, and refrigerate until ready to use. The syrup will keep in the refrigerator, for up to 2 weeks.

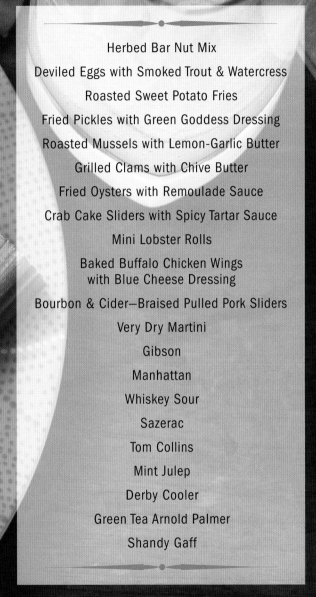

CHAPTER 2

american bar classics

herbed bar nut mix

IT'S A NICE TREAT TO TAKE A SEAT AT THE BAR AND HAVE THE BARTENDER OFFER SOMETHING DELICIOUS TO NIBBLE on while you consider your drink order. I especially like a salty, crunchy snack, like these roasted nuts made with fresh herbs and a hint of brown sugar. These disappear fast at my house, so you may want to double the recipe.

Makes 3 cups

1 cup unsalted raw cashews

1 cup unsalted pecans

1 cup walnuts

2 tablespoons unsalted butter

2 tablespoons light brown sugar

**2 tablespoons chopped
   fresh rosemary**

**1 tablespoon chopped
   fresh thyme leaves**

Pinch of cayenne pepper

**Kosher salt and freshly ground
   black pepper**

Preheat the oven to 350°F. Put the nuts in a large bowl.

Melt the butter in a small saucepan over medium heat. Add the brown sugar, rosemary, thyme, cayenne pepper, and salt and pepper to taste, and cook, stirring, until combined. Pour the mixture over the nuts, and toss well.

Spread the nuts out on a large, rimmed baking sheet, and bake for 10 minutes. Toss the nuts with a spatula, and bake for 5 more minutes. Remove from the oven, sprinkle the nuts with additional salt and pepper, and let sit until cool, 10 to 15 minutes. The nuts will keep in an airtight container for up to one week.

deviled eggs with smoked trout & watercress

DEVILED EGGS ARE A DELICIOUS BAR FARE STAPLE, AND THEY ARE GOOD ACCOMPANIMENTS TO A VARIETY OF DRINKS. Whenever I serve this tasty version made with smoked trout and peppery fresh watercress, they disappear from the table very quickly.

Makes one dozen

6 large eggs

½ cup mayonnaise

1 teaspoon Dijon mustard

¼ teaspoon smoked paprika

3 tablespoons crumbled smoked trout, skin and bones removed

2 tablespoons chopped fresh watercress, plus whole sprigs for garnish

Kosher salt and freshly ground black pepper

Put the eggs in a large saucepan and add cold water to cover. Bring to a gentle boil over medium-high heat. When the water just begins to boil, remove the pot from the heat and cover tightly. Let the eggs stand, covered, for 10 minutes. Drain the eggs and rinse them under cold running water. Pat the eggs dry and let them cool completely.

When the eggs are cool enough to handle, peel them, and cut them in half lengthwise. Gently scoop the yolks into a large bowl, being careful not to break the whites. Arrange the egg white halves, cavity-side up, on a platter, and set aside.

Mash the egg yolks with a fork, stir in the mayonnaise, mustard, and paprika, and mix until smooth. Stir in the trout and chopped watercress, and blend well. Add salt and pepper to taste.

Using a small spoon, mound the filling in the cavities of the egg white halves, dividing it evenly. The deviled eggs may be refrigerated for up to 3 hours before serving. Top each egg half with a sprig of watercress, and serve chilled.

roasted sweet potato fries

SALTY ROASTED SWEET POTATOES WITH HINTS OF FRESH THYME, HOT SMOKED PAPRIKA, AND CINNAMON MAKE an excellent bar nosh. These taste great with a bourbon or Scotch drink.

Serves 4 to 6

6 medium sweet potatoes, halved and cut into 3-inch wedges

2 tablespoons olive oil

½ teaspoon hot smoked paprika

½ teaspoon ground cinnamon

1 tablespoon crumbled fresh thyme leaves

Kosher salt

Preheat the oven to 350°F.

Put the sweet potatoes in a large bowl. Add the olive oil, paprika, and cinnamon, and gently toss together to coat evenly. Spread the sweet potatoes on a baking sheet, and sprinkle them with the thyme and salt to taste. Roast in the oven until just crisp, about 1½ hours. Sprinkle with additional salt if desired, and let cool a bit before serving.

fried pickles with green goddess dressing

FRIED PICKLES WERE NEW TO ME, AND I THOUGHT THEY SOUNDED A BIT LIKE FAIR FOOD (IN THE VEIN OF FRIED Oreos). But when I first tasted them, I was pleasantly surprised by their subtle and savory flavor.

Serves 4

Vegetable oil, for frying

1 cup unbleached, all-purpose flour

Kosher salt and freshly ground black pepper

2 cups sliced dill pickles (24 to 30 pickles), drained and patted dry

1 egg

½ cup buttermilk

1 cup panko breadcrumbs

Green Goddess Dressing (recipe follows), for serving

Pour the oil in a skillet to a depth of about ½-inch, and heat over medium heat until hot but not smoking.

Combine the flour and salt and pepper to taste in a large zip-top plastic bag. Add the pickles, and shake to coat. In a small bowl, whisk the egg and buttermilk together. Put the panko crumbs on a plate.

Dip the flour-coated pickles into the egg mixture, then dredge in the panko crumbs. Repeat with the remaining pickles.

Drop the pickles, a few at a time, in the hot oil, and cook for 1 minute. Turn, and cook for an additional minute until golden brown. Drain on paper towels. Serve with Green Goddess Dressing.

green goddess dressing

Makes about ¾ cup

2 tablespoons chopped fresh parsley

2 tablespoons chopped fresh chives

2 tablespoons chopped scallions, white and green parts

1 tablespoon chopped fresh tarragon leaves

½ cup mayonnaise

2 tablespoons sour cream or crème fraiche

1 tablespoon white vinegar

1 tablespoon fresh lemon juice

Put the parsley, chives, scallions, and tarragon in a food processor, and pulse until finely chopped. Add the mayonnaise, sour cream, vinegar, and lemon juice, and pulse until smooth. Taste, and adjust the seasonings, if necessary. Chill in the refrigerator, covered, for at least 2 hours or up to 2 days before serving.

roasted mussels with lemon-garlic butter

I AM ALWAYS LOOKING FOR NEW WAYS TO COOK MUSSELS, AND THIS RECIPE IS A REAL WINNER. THE DELICIOUS Lemon-Garlic Butter can be used in any number of other dishes, too. Put a platter of these down on your cocktail table, and watch them disappear.

Serves 6 to 8

2 pounds medium-sized mussels (about 48), rinsed and scrubbed

½ cup plus 1 tablespoon dry white wine, divided

6 tablespoons (¾ stick) unsalted butter

1 tablespoon finely minced garlic

1 tablespoon finely chopped fresh flat-leaf parsley

1 tablespoon finely chopped fresh chives

1 tablespoon fresh lemon juice

Kosher salt and freshly ground black pepper

½ cup panko breadcrumbs

Lemon wedges

Put the mussels and ½ cup of the wine wine in a large stockpot, and bring to a boil over medium-high heat. Cover and cook until the mussels open, 5 to 7 minutes. Drain and discard any mussels that do not open. Let cool a bit.

Line a large baking sheet with tin foil. Break each mussel shell at the hinge, discard one half of the shell, and arrange the mussels in the remaining halves on the baking sheet.

Melt the butter in a small sauté pan over medium heat. Add the garlic, and cook for 1 minute. Add the parsley, chives, remaining tablespoon of wine, and lemon juice, and cook, stirring, for 5 minutes. Add salt and pepper to taste.

Preheat the oven to 450°F. Spoon the butter over the mussels. Sprinkle the breadcrumbs evenly over the mussels. Roast the mussels in the oven until the breadcrumbs are golden brown, about 10 minutes. Garnish with lemon wedges, and serve at once.

grilled clams with chive butter

HERE IS A SIMPLE SEAFOOD PREPARATION TO MAKE ON THE GRILL. WHEN CLAMS ARE GRILLED, THEY BECOME deliciously smoky, and with a drizzle of fresh chive butter, they make a wonderful snack to enjoy with a drink before dinner. Serve with small cocktail forks and plenty of napkins.

Serves 6 to 8

2 dozen littleneck or cherrystone clams (see Note)

½ cup (1 stick) unsalted butter

2 tablespoons minced fresh chives

Lemon wedges, for serving

Prepare a medium-hot fire in a charcoal or gas grill. Grill the clams in a grill pan or directly on the grill grate (if small enough) until the clams open, about 5 minutes depending on size. Discard any clams that do not open. Remove to a platter with a spatula or a slotted spoon.

In a saucepan, melt the butter over medium-low heat. Add the chives, and stir. Drizzle the butter over the clams, and serve at once with lemon wedges.

Note: Littleneck clams are smaller than cherrystones, and their flavor is a bit sweeter. Their cooking time will be shorter than cherrystones.

fried oysters with remoulade sauce

I'M A BIG FAN OF OYSTER BARS, AND WHEN I SEE FRIED OYSTERS ON THE MENU, I ALWAYS ORDER THEM. HERE'S an easy recipe to make at home for "crispy on the outside—juicy on the inside" fried oysters.

Serves 6

½ **cup unbleached white flour**

1 cup yellow cornmeal

¼ **teaspoon cayenne pepper**

¼ **teaspoon paprika**

Kosher salt and freshly ground black pepper

3 dozen (3 pints) large shucked oysters, drained

Safflower oil, for frying

Remoulade Sauce (recipe follows), for serving

Put the flour in a small bowl. Combine the cornmeal, cayenne pepper, paprika, and salt and pepper to taste in a larger bowl, and blend well.

Drain the oysters. Dredge them in the flour, then in the cornmeal mixture, shaking off any excess.

Pour the oil in a skillet to a depth of about 1 inch, and heat over medium heat until hot but not smoking. Drop the oysters, a few at a time, in the hot oil; cook, stirring often with a slotted spoon, until golden brown all over, about 2 minutes. Do not overcook. Remove and drain on paper towels. Serve with Remoulade Sauce.

remoulade sauce

Makes ¾ cup

⅔ cup mayonnaise

1 tablespoon Dijon mustard

2 scallions, white and green parts, trimmed and minced

2 tablespoons finely minced fresh flat-leaf parsley

1 teaspoon fresh lemon juice

1 teaspoon Worcestershire sauce

1 teaspoon sweet paprika

Dash of hot pepper sauce

Kosher salt and freshly ground black pepper

In a bowl, whisk together the mayonnaise, mustard, scallions, parsley, lemon juice, Worcestershire sauce, paprika, hot pepper sauce, and salt and pepper to taste until well blended. Taste, and adjust the seasonings as necessary. The sauce will keep in the refrigerator, covered, for up to 1 day. Bring to room temperature before using.

crab cake sliders with spicy tartar sauce

THE TRICK TO PREPARING THESE CRAB CAKES IS TO REFRIGERATE THEM FOR AT LEAST AN HOUR BEFORE FRYING them, so plan accordingly.

Makes 12 sliders

1 pound lump crabmeat, picked over

1 tablespoon fresh lemon juice

½ cup plain bread crumbs

1 large egg

5 tablespoons mayonnaise

2 scallions, finely minced

1 tablespoon chopped fresh parsley

1 tablespoon dry mustard

Salt and freshly ground black pepper

2 tablespoons unsalted butter

2 tablespoons canola or safflower oil, divided

12 slider rolls

Spicy Tartar Sauce (recipe follows)

2 cups mixed salad greens

Put the crabmeat in a bowl, sprinkle with the lemon juice, and gently toss.

In a large bowl, mix together the bread crumbs, egg, mayonnaise, scallions, parsley, mustard, and salt and pepper to taste. Add the crabmeat, and mix together gently.

Shape into small patties, about 1 inch thick and 2 inches wide, and transfer to a baking sheet. Cover with plastic wrap, and refrigerate for at least an hour.

Heat 1 tablespoon each of the butter and oil in a large skillet, and cook half of the crab cakes until golden, 3 to 5 minutes per side. Drain on paper towels. Heat the remaining butter and oil, and repeat with the rest of the crab cakes.

To assemble the sliders, put the crab cakes on the rolls, spread them with the tartar sauce, top with greens, and serve at once.

spicy tartar sauce

Makes about 1 cup

¾ cup mayonnaise

2 tablespoons chopped fresh cilantro

2 tablespoons chopped fresh parsley

¼ cup sweet pickle relish

8 dashes hot sauce

2 tablespoons fresh lime juice

1 tablespoon chili powder

1 tablespoon ground cumin

**Kosher salt and freshly ground
    black pepper**

To make the tartar sauce, combine the mayonnaise, cilantro, parsley, relish, hot sauce, lime juice, chili powder, cumin, and salt and pepper to taste in a medium bowl, and mix well. The sauce will keep in the refrigerator, covered, for up to 3 days.

mini lobster rolls

LOBSTER ROLLS HAVE BECOME WILDLY POPULAR IN RECENT YEARS, AND FOR GOOD REASON—THEY ARE SUBLIME summer food. They can be prepared with melted butter or light vinaigrette, but my favorite version is lobster salad made with mayonnaise and chopped celery. Although plain, toasted hot dog rolls are fine to serve with the lobster, brioche rolls take them to a new level.

Makes 12 mini rolls

3 cups lobster meat, picked over (see Note)

3 celery ribs, diced

¼ cup chopped fresh flat-leaf parsley

¾ cup mayonnaise

1 teaspoon Dijon mustard

1 tablespoon fresh lemon juice

½ teaspoon paprika

Kosher salt and freshly ground black pepper

6 plain hot dog or brioche rolls

2 tablespoons unsalted butter, at room temperature (optional)

Put the lobster meat, celery, and parsley in a large bowl.

Put the mayonnaise, mustard, lemon juice, paprika, and salt and pepper to taste in a bowl, and mix well to combine. Fold into the lobster, and mix well.

Toast the rolls in a warm oven or toaster oven until golden brown, being careful not to burn them. Spread them with butter, if desired. Spoon the lobster into each roll, cut in half crosswise, and serve at once.

Note: A 1¼ pound cooked lobster yields about 1 cup of lobster meat. Save the lobster shells, and simmer them with onions and herbs to make a great-tasting, briny lobster stock that is a perfect base for seafood soups or for poaching fish or shellfish.

buffalo chicken wings with blue cheese dressing

BUFFALO CHICKEN WINGS WERE INVENTED IN 1964 AT THE ANCHOR BAR IN BUFFALO, NEW YORK, AND THEY HAVE been the quintessential bar snack ever since. They are often fiery hot with blue cheese dip and celery sticks on the side: it's an odd combination, but it works. My own version of wings is oven-baked—not fried—and they are medium-hot and fairly sweet. You can serve them with extra hot sauce for those who prefer a hotter wing. As one who has Buffalo roots, I can tell you that to make authentic Buffalo wings, you must use Frank's Hot Sauce—no substitutes, no kidding.

Serves 4 to 6

**12 whole chicken wings
(2¼ to 2½ pounds)**

2 tablespoons olive oil

3 garlic cloves, thinly sliced

**Kosher salt and freshly ground
black pepper**

½ stick unsalted butter

**⅓ cup Frank's Hot Sauce,
plus more for serving**

1 tablespoon honey

**Blue Cheese Dressing
(recipe follows), for serving**

24 celery sticks, for serving

Preheat the oven to 425°F. Using a sharp knife or kitchen shears, separate the wings at the joint.

In a large bowl, toss the wings with the olive oil, garlic, and salt and pepper to taste. Arrange the wings in a single layer in a baking pan, and bake until just done, turning once, 25 minutes.

Meanwhile, melt the butter in small saucepan over medium heat. Add the hot sauce and honey, and stir to combine. Transfer to a large bowl.

Remove the wings from the oven, and toss them with the hot sauce mixture until they are well-coated. Return them to the baking pan, and bake for an additional 10 minutes.

Serve with Blue Cheese Dressing, celery sticks, and additional hot sauce.

blue cheese dressing

Makes about 1 cup

½ cup mayonnaise

½ cup buttermilk

1 tablespoon white wine vinegar

**½ cup crumbled blue cheese
(about 2 ounces)**

**Kosher salt and freshly ground
black pepper**

In a medium bowl, whisk together the mayonnaise, buttermilk, and vinegar until smooth. Add the blue cheese, crumbling with a fork, if necessary, until well-combined. Add salt and pepper to taste, and chill in the refrigerator for 2 hours. The dressing can be made up to 3 days ahead of time.

bourbon & cider–braised pulled pork sliders

SLOW-COOKED PORK SLIDERS MAKE WONDERFUL PARTY FOOD FOR A HUNGRY CROWD, AND THEY FIT THE BILL
if you want to serve something that's a bit more substantial than a bar snack.

Makes 16 sliders

3 to 3½ pounds pork shoulder

1 tablespoon kosher salt

2 tablespoons brown sugar

¼ teaspoon cayenne pepper

1 teaspoon smoked paprika

1 tablespoon corn oil

2 onions, chopped

1½ cups apple cider

¼ cup bourbon

¼ cup apple cider vinegar

1 tablespoon Dijon mustard

Dash hot sauce

Kosher salt and freshly ground
   black pepper

16 slider rolls or 8 regular
   hamburger rolls, split

Pat the pork dry. In a small bowl, stir together the salt, brown sugar, cayenne pepper, and paprika. Rub the mixture all over the pork, wrap in plastic wrap, and let marinate in the refrigerator for at least 4 hours or up to overnight.

Preheat the oven to 375°F. In a Dutch oven, sear the pork on all sides. Remove the pork from the pot, and set aside. Drain off the fat, and return the pot to the heat.

Add the oil to the pot, and cook the onions over medium heat until softened, scraping up the browned bits from the bottom. Add the cider, and bring to a low simmer. Remove from the heat, add the pork back to the pot, cover, and put in the oven. Braise the pork for 4 hours, basting and turning occasionally, until an instant-read thermometer reads 175°F.

Remove the pork from the pot, and transfer to a cutting board to cool a bit. Using two forks, shred the meat off the bone.

Add the bourbon, vinegar, and mustard to the pot. Simmer, stirring occasionally, for 5 minutes. Add the shredded pork, and continue cooking until most of the liquid is absorbed. Add hot sauce and salt and pepper to taste.

Divide the pulled pork evenly among the slider rolls. If using regular hamburger rolls, cut each sandwich in half. Serve at once.

american bar classics

∷∷∷∷∷∷∷

COCKTAILS

very dry martini

A DRY MARTINI IS TRADITIONALLY MADE WITH GIN, ALTHOUGH VODKA IS THE PREFERRED SPIRIT OF MANY MARTINI drinkers. For a very cold martini, shake it instead of stirring. Serve with a green olive or a twist of lemon. End of story.

Serves 1

Splash of dry vermouth

2 ounces gin or vodka

Green olive or lemon twist

Stirring Method: Fill a mixing glass with ice. Add the vermouth and gin or vodka, and stir. Strain into a chilled martini glass.

Shaking Method: Fill a shaker with ice. Add the vermouth and gin or vodka, and shake well. Strain into a chilled martini glass.

Garnish with an olive or a lemon twist, and serve.

gibson

A GIBSON IS BASICALLY A DRY MARTINI THAT IS GARNISHED WITH A COCKTAIL ONION INSTEAD OF THE USUAL OLIVE or twist. I know this because it is my husband's preferred drink. Recently, we were having a cocktail at the bar at Fort Defiance in Red Hook, Brooklyn, and he was served a Gibson that was made with delicious house-pickled onions. It was a revelation. Pickled onions (page 12) are simple to make, and we now always have a jar of them in our refrigerator. Garnish a Gibson (or any other drink) with a few of them, and you will never go back to the store-bought kind again.

Serves 1

Splash of dry vermouth

2 ounces gin or vodka

**Pickled Cocktail Onions
(page 12), for garnish**

Stirring Method: Fill a mixing glass with ice. Add the vermouth and gin or vodka, and stir. Strain into a chilled martini glass.

Shaking Method: Fill a shaker with ice. Add vermouth and gin or vodka, and shake well. Strain into a chilled martini glass.

Garnish with 2 or 3 cocktail onions, and serve.

manhattan

MANHATTANS HAVE A SMOOTH AND MELLOW TASTE, AND THEY GO WELL WITH SOMETHING SALTY TO NIBBLE on before dinner. Garnish this cocktail with a Marinated Fresh Cherry (page 12), which is nothing like the bright red maraschino cherries available at the supermarket.

Serves 1

2 ounces whiskey (rye or bourbon)

1 ounce sweet vermouth

2 dashes Angostura bitters

1 Marinated Fresh Cherry (page 12), for garnish

Fill a mixing glass with ice. Add the whiskey, vermouth, and bitters, and stir well. Strain into a chilled cocktail glass. Garnish with a cherry, and serve.

Variation: For a Dry Manhattan, substitute dry vermouth for sweet vermouth, and garnish with a lemon twist.

whiskey sour

THIS CLASSIC COCKTAIL IS ONE FROM MY PARENTS' GENERATION, WHEN IT WAS A VERY POPULAR DRINK TO SERVE before Sunday lunch or a dinner party. Whiskey Sours can be made with whiskey or bourbon, and they sometimes include egg whites to make them frothy, but I prefer them without.

Serves 1

½ ounce fresh lemon juice

1 teaspoon simple syrup
  (page 13) or granulated sugar

1½ ounces whiskey or bourbon

1 orange slice, for garnish

1 Marinated Fresh Cherry (page 12),
  for garnish

Fill a cocktail shaker with ice. Add the lemon juice, simple syrup, and whiskey, shake well until very cold, and strain into a chilled stemmed glass. Garnish with an orange slice and a cherry, and serve.

sazerac

THE SAZERAC COCKTAIL ORIGINATED IN NEW ORLEANS IN THE 1830S. ANTOINE PEYCHAUD, A CREOLE PHARMACIST who created Peychaud's Bitters, first made the drink with brandy, absinthe, and his own bitters. It got its name from the owner of the Sazerac Coffee House, where it was made exclusively with Sazerac de Forge et Fils brandy. This vintage New Orleans cocktail pairs well with rich bar snacks, such as Deviled Eggs with Smoked Trout & Watercress (page 19) or Crab Cake Sliders (page 28).

Serves 1

Splash of Absinthe or Herbsaint

2 ounces rye whiskey

½ ounce simple syrup
  (page 13)

2 dashes Peychaud's bitters

Lemon or orange peel, for garnish

Chill one rocks glass while preparing the drink in another. Splash the Herbsaint into the second glass, and swirl it to coat the glass, then pour it out. Add the rye, simple syrup, and bitters, and stir with an ice cube to chill. Strain into the chilled rocks glass. Garnish with a lemon or orange peel, and serve.

tom collins

THIS IS A VERY PLEASANT, LEMONY SUMMER SIPPER THAT GOES DOWN EASILY WITH A VARIETY OF COCKTAIL snacks. It was originally made with Old Tom gin, hence the name. you may want to mix this drink with other spirits—with rum it becomes a Rum Collins, and with bourbon or whiskey, it is called a John Collins. Whatever you call it, it is incredibly refreshing.

Serves 1

¾ ounce fresh lemon juice

1 teaspoon simple syrup (page 13) or granulated sugar

1½ ounces gin

About 2 ounces club soda or seltzer

1 lemon slice, for garnish

Pour the lemon juice and simple syrup into a highball glass, and stir until the sugar dissolves (if using). Add ice to fill the glass halfway. Add the gin, and stir. Fill with club soda. Garnish with a lemon slice, and serve.

Derby Cooler

mint julep

THE KEY TO MAKING A GOOD MINT JULEP IS TO USE DECENT BOURBON AND VERY FRESH MINT. INVITE YOUR FRIENDS over to watch the Kentucky Derby, and serve these classic Southern cocktails with a batch of Fried Oysters (page 26).

Serves 1

2 sprigs fresh mint

½ ounce simple syrup (page 13) or 1 teaspoon granulated sugar

2 ounces bourbon

Crushed ice

In the bottom of a highball glass or a chilled julep cup, gently bruise one sprig of mint with the simple syrup. Add half of the bourbon, and fill the glass halfway with crushed ice. Stir with a long spoon until the outside of the glass frosts. Add more crushed ice and the remaining bourbon to fill the glass. Stir again to frost, garnish with the remaining mint sprig, and serve.

derby cooler

IF YOU WANT TO TRY SOMETHING DIFFERENT ON DERBY DAY, HERE IS A WONDERFULLY REFRESHING COCKTAIL THAT is infused with ginger syrup and garnished with fresh mint. Whether you watch the horse race or not, it's a perfect warm-weather quaff to slowly sip and savor.

Serves 1

1½ ounces bourbon

2 ounces grapefruit juice

1 tablespoon ginger syrup (page 15)

½ ounce fresh lemon juice

Club soda or seltzer

Dash of Peychaud bitters

1 large sprig fresh mint

Fill a cocktail shaker with ice and add the bourbon, grapefruit juice, ginger syrup, and lemon juice: shake well. Strain into an old-fashioned glass filled with ice. Top off with the soda, and add the bitters. Garnish with the mint sprig, and serve.

green tea arnold palmer

TRY THIS COOL CONCOCTION THAT IS A SPIKED RIFF ON THE WELL-KNOWN BLEND OF ICED TEA AND LEMONADE named after golfer Arnold Palmer. Make a pot of green tea, and give it plenty of time to chill in the refrigerator. Whether you're relaxing at the 19th hole or just putting your feet up after a long day, it will hit the spot.

Serves 1

3 ounces chilled green tea

3 ounces lemonade

1½ ounces vodka

1 lemon wedge, for garnish

Fill a large rocks glass with ice. Add the tea, lemonade, and vodka. Stir with a long spoon. Garnish with a lemon wedge and serve.

shandy gaff

COCKTAILS MIXED WITH BEER ARE BECOMING VERY TRENDY IN BARS ALL OVER THE COUNTRY, BUT ONE THAT'S been around for a long time—the Shandy Gaff—is still the real deal. It's a very tasty drink to serve with Fried Pickles (page 22)!

Serves 1

1 part ginger ale or ginger beer

1 part light ale or Pilsener beer

Fill a tall glass with ice. Pour equal amounts of ginger ale and beer over the ice, and serve.

Green Tea Arnold Palmer

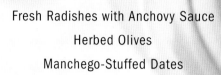

CHAPTER 3

continental tastes

fresh radishes with anchovy sauce

LOOK FOR CRISP AND PEPPERY RADISHES AT THE FARMERS' MARKET IN EARLY SUMMER WHEN THEY ARE FRESH and abundant. Like many fresh vegetables, they taste terrific with a light anchovy sauce—they're also excellent with softened sweet butter and sea salt.

Serves 6 to 8

2 bunches radishes, tops trimmed and left on

Sea salt and freshly ground black pepper

3 salt-packed anchovies

2 garlic cloves, peeled

Pinch of crushed red pepper flakes

1 teaspoon Dijon mustard

1 teaspoon red wine vinegar

1 teaspoon fresh lemon juice

¼ cup extra-virgin olive oil

Rinse the radishes well, and pat dry. Slice them in half, arrange them on a platter, and sprinkle with salt and pepper to taste.

Chop the anchovies, and put them in a bowl. Smash the garlic with the side of a knife, and add it to the bowl. Work the anchovies and the garlic into a smooth paste with a fork or the back of a spoon. Add the pepper flakes, mustard, vinegar, and lemon juice, and mix well. Whisk in the olive oil. The sauce can also be prepared in a blender.

Serve as a dipping sauce with the radishes.

herbed olives

SOME EVENINGS, YOU MAY JUST WANT TO PUT OUT A SIMPLE PLATTER OF FRESH VEGETABLES DRIZZLED WITH GOOD olive oil or a spoonful of lively anchovy sauce, a bowl of meaty olives, and some good bread. I always have a jar of herbed olives—a mixture of olives, fresh herbs, and good olive oil—on hand in the refrigerator. They taste wonderful and look beautiful. If you have other fresh herbs, such as thyme, tarragon, or marjoram, in your garden or window box, feel free to try them. This preparation of Herbed Olives (plus the Fresh Radishes with Anchovy Sauce on page 46) accompanies a few rounds of cocktails quite nicely.

Makes about 1 pint

4 teaspoons black or multicolored peppercorns

1 tablespoon crushed fresh rosemary

1 teaspoon crushed red pepper flakes

1 teaspoon fennel seeds

3 cups mixed olives (about 1 pound), drained if necessary

1½ cups extra-virgin olive oil

2 bay leaves

2 garlic cloves, crushed

In a small bowl, mix together the peppercorns, rosemary, pepper flakes, and fennel seeds. Add the olives, and toss to coat and mix. Add the olive oil, bay leaves, and garlic; toss again to coat, then cover and refrigerate for at least 2 hours and up to 2 weeks. Let the olives come to room temperature before serving.

manchego-stuffed dates

THIS IS A FAVORITE OF TAPAS BARS, AND MANY PLACES SERVE THEIR OWN VERSIONS MADE WITH A VARIETY OF different cheeses and prosciutto or Serrano ham. I particularly like making it with Manchego cheese and bacon. It would be hard to go wrong with any combination.

Makes 1 dozen

12 Medjool dates

3 ounces Manchego cheese

4 slices bacon,
  each cut into 3 segments

Preheat the oven to 425°F. Line a baking sheet with aluminum foil.

Cut a lengthwise slit into each date, and remove the pit. Cut the cheese into strips to fit inside the dates. Stuff each date with the cheese, and pinch closed.

Wrap each date with a piece of bacon, and secure with a toothpick. Arrange the dates on the prepared baking sheet, seam side down.

Bake for 6 minutes. Remove from the oven, and using tongs, carefully turn the dates. Return to the oven, and bake until browned and crisp, about 6 minutes longer. Serve warm or at room temperature.

Note: The dates can be prepared up to 3 hours before baking. Cover, and refrigerate until ready to bake.

onion & gruyère tart

THIS TART—MADE WITH SLOW-COOKED ONIONS BAKED INTO A BUTTERY CRUST WITH GRUYÈRE CHEESE AND
fresh thyme—is fantastic. I like to cut it into thin wedges and serve it warm with Lillet Coolers (page 65).

Serves 6 to 8

1 cup all-purpose flour

Pinch of salt

**6 tablespoons unsalted butter,
chilled, cut in ¼-inch cubes**

3 to 6 tablespoons ice water

2 tablespoons olive oil

**2 pounds yellow onions, peeled
and thinly sliced**

Kosher salt

2 tablespoons Marsala wine

Freshly ground black pepper

**2 ounces finely grated Gruyère
cheese, divided**

**1 teaspoon fresh thyme leaves,
plus extra for garnish**

1 egg, lightly beaten

Put the flour, salt, and butter in a food processor. Pulse until the mixture resembles coarse meal. Add the water, a tablespoon at a time, until the dough comes together. Form into a ball, and flatten. Wrap in plastic wrap, and refrigerate for 1 hour.

Preheat the oven to 375°F.

Heat the olive oil in a large skillet over medium heat. Add the onions, season to taste with salt, and cook, stirring occasionally, until softened and golden brown, about 30 minutes. Add the wine and black pepper to taste and cook, stirring for 2 minutes. Remove the onions from the heat and let cool.

Roll out the dough to fit in a 10-inch tart pan with a removable bottom. Fit the dough into the pan, press it into the fluted edges, and trim off the excess pastry. Prick the bottom of the dough all over with a fork and line the pan with foil. Fill the pan with pie weights or dried beans and bake for 10 minutes, until the exposed crust edges are lightly browned. Remove the foil and weights, prick the crust with a fork, and return the pan to the oven for 5 minutes, just until the bottom of the tart is dry. Remove and let cool.

Sprinkle half of the cheese over the bottom of the tart. Spoon the onions into the shell, and spread evenly. Sprinkle the thyme over the onions. Brush the exposed crust rim with the egg wash. Sprinkle the tart with the remaining cheese.

Bake until the crust is firm and lightly browned and the onions are golden brown, about 30 minutes. Remove, and let cool slightly. Garnish with thyme sprigs, and serve warm or at room temperature.

tomato bread

TOMATO BREAD *(PAN CON TOMATE)* IS A STAPLE IN TAPAS BARS ALL OVER SPAIN. IT IS SIMPLY GRILLED BREAD THAT is rubbed with fresh garlic and tomatoes. It is delicious on its own, but you may want to kick it up a notch and serve it with a Spanish cheese—like Mahón, Cabrales, or Manchego—and Serrano ham.

Serves 4 to 6

¼ cup extra-virgin olive oil, divided

1 baguette, split in half lengthwise then cut into 4 equal sections

2 large garlic cloves, halved lengthwise

4 ripe tomatoes, halved crosswise

Kosher salt and freshly ground black pepper

Lightly oil a grill pan with 1 tablespoon of the olive oil (see Note). Grill the bread in batches over medium heat until grill marks appear, 1 to 2 minutes per side.

Remove the bread from the heat, and rub 1 cut side of each slice with the cut side of the garlic half, then rub with the cut side of a tomato half, using 1 tomato half for 2 slices of the bread. Brush the bread with olive oil, and sprinkle generously with salt and pepper. Serve at once.

Note: The bread can also be prepared on a gas or charcoal grill over medium heat.

taleggio & swiss chard crostini

TALEGGIO, A SEMI-SOFT CHEESE FROM THE LOMBARDY REGION OF ITALY, HAS A WONDERFULLY PUNGENT FLAVOR, and it is especially delicious when melted. For a superb appetizer, bake it on crusty sourdough bread and top with sautéed Swiss chard.

Serves 6 to 8

- 1 sourdough baguette or loaf of ciabatta bread, cut on the diagonal into ¾-inch slices
- 8 ounces Taleggio cheese
- 1 pound Swiss chard, rinsed and stemmed
- 2 tablespoons olive oil
- 2 garlic cloves, thinly sliced
- Pinch of red pepper flakes
- Kosher salt and freshly ground black pepper

Preheat the oven to 350°F. Put the bread slices on a baking sheet.

Remove the rind from the cheese, cut it into pieces that will fit on the bread slices, and arrange them on the bread. Bake in the oven until the cheese is melted and bubby, about 10 minutes.

Meanwhile, chop the chard leaves into ½-inch strips. Heat the olive oil in a large sauté pan over medium heat. Add the garlic, and cook until fragrant, but do not let it brown. Add the chard, red pepper flakes, and salt and pepper to taste, and toss to mix. Reduce the heat to low, cover, and cook for about 10 minutes. Toss occasionally, until the leaves are wilted and turn dark green. Transfer the greens with a slotted spoon to a bowl.

Arrange the cheesy bread on a platter, top each slice with a generous amount of chard, and serve at once.

bruschetta with ricotta cheese, spinach & prosciutto

BRUSCHETTA IS ONE OF MY GO-TO DISHES TO SERVE AT PARTIES, AND IT IS PROOF THAT SIMPLE FOOD DOESN'T necessarily mean unsophisticated food. It can be prepared on a charcoal grill, in a grill pan, or in the oven. Cook as many slices as will fit in a single layer, and turn them only once, until they are golden brown and crispy. This is one of my favorite versions of bruschetta.

Makes one dozen

6 (½-inch) slices sourdough or country bread, or ciabatta

3 large garlic cloves, peeled and halved

½ cup plus 1 tablespoon olive oil, divided

3 cups packed baby spinach, rinsed and patted dry

Kosher salt and freshly ground black pepper

Pinch of dried chile flakes

¾ cup good quality ricotta cheese, at room temperature

12 very thin slices prosciutto

Prepare a grill pan over medium heat. Grill the bread slices in a single layer, turning once, until they are golden brown and crispy, and slightly charred around the edges, 3 to 5 minutes. Remove from the heat. Rub the garlic halves over one side of the bread, and brush lightly with ½ cup of the olive oil. Cut each slice in half.

Alternatively, to prepare bruschetta in the oven, preheat the oven to 450°F. Arrange the bread slices in a single layer on a baking sheet, and bake until golden brown and crispy, 6 to 8 minutes. Remove from the heat. Rub the garlic halves over one side of the bread, then brush lightly with the ½ cup of the olive oil. Cut each slice in half.

Meanwhile, heat the remaining tablespoon of olive oil in a skillet or sauté pan. Add the spinach and sauté until wilted, about 3 minutes. Season to taste with salt and pepper, add the chile flakes, and sauté for 1 minute. Drain the spinach, and transfer to a bowl.

Spread the bruschetta slices with the ricotta cheese, top with the cooked spinach and a slice of prosciutto, and serve at once.

pizza with mozzarella, roasted cherry tomatoes & pancetta

HERE IS A FANTASTIC VERSION OF HOMEMADE PIZZA THAT YOU WILL WANT TO SERVE TO FRIENDS WITH A ROUND or two of drinks. The dough is really a free-form tart dough that doesn't require much rising time, and you can make it a day ahead. Look for a mix of red and yellow cherry tomatoes to make your pizza look even more beautiful.

Serves 4 to 6

Pizza Dough:

1 teaspoon active dry yeast

½ cup lukewarm water (about 110°F)

1½ cups all-purpose unbleached flour, divided

½ teaspoon kosher salt

1½ tablespoons melted butter

Topping:

6 garlic cloves, thinly sliced

2 cups ripe mixed cherry tomatoes, halved

2 tablespoons olive oil

2 cups shredded mozzarella cheese (about 8 ounces)

4 ounces thinly sliced pancetta

½ cup freshly grated Parmesan cheese, for garnish

¼ cup fresh basil leaves, for garnish

For the dough: In a mixing bowl, dissolve the yeast in the water. Stir in ¼ cup of the flour, and let the mixture get bubbly, about 15 minutes. Add the salt, butter, and the remaining flour, and mix to form a ball. Knead the dough for about 5 minutes. Put the dough in a large bowl, cover with a damp towel or plastic wrap, and let it rise until doubled in size, about 1 hour. (Or, put the dough in a large zip-top plastic bag, and let it rise for several hours or overnight.)

For the topping: Preheat the oven to 350°F. Arrange the garlic and tomatoes on a baking sheet. Pour the oil over the top and toss to coat evenly. Roast the tomatoes until just softened, 15 to 20 minutes. Remove from the oven, and let cool.

Raise the heat to 375°F. Punch down the dough, and knead it into a smooth ball. Roll out the dough to an oval about 11 inches by 15 inches, and transfer to a baking sheet lined with parchment.

Scatter the mozzarella evenly over the dough, and spread the roasted tomato mixture over the cheese. Bake for 30 to 35 minutes, until the pizza is nicely browned. Cool on a rack for a few minutes.

Meanwhile, cook the pancetta in a dry skillet until just crisp. Drain on paper towels, and cut into small pieces.

Sprinkle the top of the pizza with the pancetta, Parmesan cheese, and basil leaves, and serve.

grilled gruyère & sun-dried tomato bites

GRILLED CHEESE SANDWICHES ARE NOT JUST FOR KIDS, AND ANYWAY, WHY SHOULD THEY HAVE ALL THE FUN? These sophisticated and hearty grilled cheese sandwich bites are delicious, savory snacks made with nutty-flavored Gruyère.

Makes 16 bites

8 slices Italian country-style, sourdough, or olive bread (about ½-inch thick)

4 tablespoons unsalted butter, at room temperature

2 cups shredded Gruyere cheese (about 8 ounces)

½ cup oil-packed sun-dried tomatoes (about 8 ounces), drained and halved

Butter one side of each slice of bread. Put 4 slices, buttered side down, on a work surface. Sprinkle the cheese and tomatoes evenly over each of and top with the remaining slices, buttered side up.

Heat a large nonstick skillet over medium heat. Cook the sandwiches in the skillet in batches. Cover until the sandwiches are golden brown on one side and the cheese has begun to melt, about 2 minutes. Turn the sandwiches with a spatula, and press to flatten them slightly. Cook until the sandwiches are golden brown on both sides and the cheese has melted completely, about another minute. Cut each sandwich into quarters, and serve at once.

smoked salmon & cucumber tea sandwiches with chive butter

I RECENTLY WENT TO AN AFTERNOON PARTY, AND THE HOSTESS SERVED TASTY, BUTTERY CUCUMBER TEA SANDWICHES. I decided to try making them with smoked salmon and watercress and butter mixed with fresh chives, and they're quite delicious. While we often think of these sandwiches as accompaniments to afternoon tea, they are also good to nibble on with a martini or Gibson (page 36), or a Pimm's Cup (page70).

Makes 16 sandwiches

¾ **stick unsalted butter,
   at room temperature**

2 **tablespoons finely minced chives**

16 **thin slices white sandwich bread,
   crusts removed**

2 **or 3 small cucumbers, peeled
   and very thinly sliced**

4 **ounces smoked salmon,
   thinly sliced**

32 **sprigs fresh watercress,
   stemmed**

In a small bowl, mix the butter and chives together with a fork. Spread the butter on one side of 8 slices of bread. Top with cucumbers, smoked salmon, and watercress. Put the remaining slices of bread on top, and gently press down on the sandwiches. Cut on the diagonal.

Serve at once, or cover and let chill in the refrigerator for up to 3 hours.

lamb & turkey meatballs with lemon-mint yogurt sauce

IF YOU DON'T WANT TO BE FRYING OVER A HOT STOVE WHILE YOUR GUESTS ARE HAVING A GREAT TIME, YOU CAN make these savory meatballs ahead of time and re-heat them in the oven. The yogurt sauce can also be made up to a day before serving. These are nice with a Campari-based drink like a Negroni (page 67) or an Americano (page 66).

Makes about 36 meatballs

¼ teaspoon ground cumin

¼ teaspoon ground coriander seeds

¼ teaspoon ground cinnamon

¼ teaspoon ground cloves

¼ teaspoon ground nutmeg

2 tablespoons finely grated
　fresh ginger

1 tablespoon minced garlic

1½ pounds ground lamb

8 ounces ground turkey or chicken

Kosher salt and freshly ground
　black pepper

1 to 2 tablespoons olive oil

Lemon-Mint Yogurt Sauce
　(recipe follows), for serving

Preheat the oven to 200°F, and line a baking sheet with paper towels.

Combine the cumin, coriander, cinnamon, cloves, and nutmeg in a small bowl, and stir together thoroughly.

In a large bowl, combine the ginger, garlic, spice mixture, lamb, turkey, and salt and pepper to taste, and mix with your hands until combined. Do not overmix. Gently roll the mixture into 1-inch balls.

Heat a large skillet over medium heat. Add 1 tablespoon of the olive oil, and swirl to coat. Brown the meatballs in batches without crowding, turning often, 10 to 12 minutes. (The meatballs can be made up to a day ahead of time. Cover, and refrigerate them. Bring to room temperature, and bake at 350°F until heated through, 15 to 20 minutes.) Transfer to the baking sheet, and keep warm in the oven.

Serve the meatballs with the yogurt sauce with toothpicks or small forks.

lemon-mint yogurt sauce

Makes about 1½ cups

1½ cups low-fat Greek yogurt

1 teaspoon lemon zest

1 tablespoon chopped fresh mint

1 tablespoon extra-virgin olive oil

½ teaspoon finely minced garlic

In a medium bowl, combine the yogurt, lemon zest, mint, olive oil, and garlic. The yogurt sauce can be made ahead and chilled for at least 2 hours or overnight before serving.

sherry-braised chorizo bites

THIS SIMPLE PREPARATION OF SPICY SPANISH CHORIZO BRAISED IN SHERRY MAKES A PERFECT SMALL BITE TO enjoy with a drink.

Serves 6

1 pound chorizo sausage

¾ cup sherry

Preheat the oven to 400°F.

Slice the sausage into ¾-inch slices. Arrange them in a baking dish, and bake until lightly browned, about 20 minutes. Remove from the oven.

Turn the sausage slices over. Pour the sherry over them. Return the sausage to the oven, and bake for 10 minutes longer.

Transfer the sausage to a plate or shallow bowl, and drizzle with a bit of the reduced sherry from the baking dish. Serve warm with toothpicks.

continental tastes

::::::::::::

COCKTAILS

French Twist

french twist

THIS IS A NICE, LIGHT COCKTAIL THAT IS MADE WITH CRÈME DE CASSIS, VERMOUTH, AND YOUR CHOICE OF gin or vodka.

Serves 1

1½ ounces gin or vodka

½ ounce dry vermouth

½ ounce crème de Cassis

1 lemon slice, for garnish

Fill a cocktail shaker with ice. Add the gin, vermouth, and crème de Cassis, and shake well. Strain into a chilled cocktail glass. Garnish with the lemon slice, and serve.

lillet cooler

LILLET (PRONOUNCED LEE-LAY) IS A FRENCH APERITIF WINE THAT IS GENERALLY SERVED ON THE ROCKS. HERE it gets a dash of grenadine and a splash of club soda to make a very refreshing cooler.

Serves 1

4 ounces Lillet Blanc

1 teaspoon grenadine

Club soda or seltzer

1 orange slice, for garnish

Fill a tall glass with ice. Add the Lillet and grenadine. Fill with club soda, and stir. Garnish with the orange slice, and serve.

americano

TO ME, THE BITTER, AROMATIC TASTE OF CAMPARI IS THE VERY ESSENCE OF ITALY, AND I HAVE FOND MEMORIES of sipping Campari cocktails at outdoor cafés in Milan, Florence, and Rome. This apertif was invented by Gaspare Campari in Milan in 1860, and it is said that the drink got its name during Prohibition, when Italian barmen noticed how much visiting Americans enjoyed it. Campari drinks go very well with bites of crostini (page 53), bruschetta (page 54), and pizza (page 56).

Serves 1

1½ ounces Campari

1½ ounces sweet vermouth

Splash of club soda or seltzer

1 twist lemon peel, for garnish

1 twist orange peel, for garnish

Fill a highball glass with ice, and add the Campari, vermouth, and a splash of club soda. Stir well, garnish with the lemon and orange peels, and serve.

negroni

ANOTHER WONDERFUL CAMPARI CONCOCTION IS THE NEGRONI. SIP THIS ONE SLOWLY—IT PACKS A WALLOP!

Serves 1

1 ounce Campari

1 ounce sweet vermouth

1 ounce gin or vodka

1 twist orange peel, for garnish

Fill a rocks glass with ice. Add the Campari, vermouth, and gin or vodka, and stir to blend. Garnish with the orange peel, and serve.

aperol spritz

APEROL IS AN ITALIAN ORANGE LIQUEUR THAT RECENTLY BECAME AVAILABLE IN THE U.S. SINCE IT ARRIVED ON the scene, the Aperol Spritz has become a wildly popular drink, and with good reason—it's light and refreshing and stimulates the appetite.

Serves 1

3 ounces Prosecco or other
   sparkling wine

1½ ounces Aperol

Splash of club soda or seltzer

1 orange slice, for garnish

Fill a highball or white wine glass ¼ full with ice. Add the Prosecco, Aperol, and a splash of club soda. Stir gently until mixed. Garnish with the orange slice, and serve.

blood orange sparkler

BLOOD ORANGE JUICE HAS A DISTINCTIVE TART AND TANGY FLAVOR THAT MIXES BEAUTIFULLY WITH VODKA. THIS festive cocktail is topped off with a splash of Prosecco, and it tastes wonderful with Herbed Olives (page 48), as well as seafood bites.

Serves 1

1 ounce vodka

2 ounces blood orange juice (see Note)

Prosecco or other sparkling wine

1 orange slice, for garnish

Fill a cocktail shaker with ice. Add the vodka and orange juice, and shake well. Strain into a chilled champagne flute. Garnish with the orange slice, and serve.

Note: If blood orange juice is not available, use fresh-squeezed navel orange juice.

aquavit bloody mary

BLOODY MARYS SPIKED WITH CARAWAY-FLAVORED AQUAVIT ARE TERRIFIC TO SERVE ALONGSIDE A SCANDINAVIAN-inspired smorgasbord. Set out a spread of rye bread, gravlax, herring, cheese, hard-boiled eggs, and pickled vegetables for a very satisfying happy hour.

Serves 6

One (46-ounce) bottle tomato juice

½ ounce fresh lemon juice

½ ounce fresh lime juice

**1 tablespoon Tabasco sauce
    or Louisiana hot sauce**

2 tablespoons prepared horseradish

1 tablespoon Worcestershire sauce

Dash of celery salt

Freshly ground black pepper

12 ounces Aquavit

**Asparagus spears, steamed and
    chilled, for garnish**

**Pickled Cocktail Onions,
    (page 12), for garnish (optional)**

Combine the tomato juice, lemon juice, lime juice, Tabasco sauce, horseradish, Worcestershire sauce, celery salt, and black pepper to taste in a large container with a tight-fitting lid. Cover tightly, and shake vigorously. The Bloody Mary mix may be made up to 3 days ahead. Chill in the refrigerator.

Fill 6 glasses with ice cubes, add 2 ounces of Aquavit to each, top off with the Bloody Mary mix, and stir. Add asparagus spears and onions for garnish, and serve.

pimm's cup

THE PIMM'S CUP IS THE QUINTESSENTIAL SUMMER DRINK IN ENGLAND. IN FACT, IT'S THE OFFICIAL DRINK OF Wimbledon. It is made with Pimm's No. 1 Cup, which is a low-alcohol, gin-based infusion of herbs and quinine. There are a number of garnishes you can add to this summery drink, but cucumber spears or slices are essential. This is lovely to drink with Smoked Salmon & Cucumber Tea Sandwiches (page 58).

Serves 1

2 ounces fresh lemon juice (juice of 1 lemon)

1 ounce simple syrup (page 13) or 1 teaspoon granulated sugar

1½ ounces Pimm's No. 1 Cup (see Note)

Club soda or seltzer

Cucumber spears or slices, plus orange, lemon, or strawberry slices, for garnish

In a tall glass, stir the lemon juice and simple syrup together. Add ice and the Pimm's. Top off with club soda, and stir. Add your desired garnishes, and serve.

Note: Look for Pimm's No. 1 Cup in the gin or liqueur and cordial sections of the liquor store.

scotch mcnelly

THIS DRINK IS A TWIST ON THE CLASSIC ROB ROY. IT'S MADE WITH PEYCHAUD'S BITTERS INSTEAD OF THE STANDARD Angostura bitters, and was named after a cool young guy that I know.

Serves 1

2 ounces scotch

1 ounce sweet vermouth

2 dashes Peychaud's bitters

1 twist lemon peel, for garnish

Fill a large glass with ice. Add the scotch, vermouth, and bitters, and stir well. Strain into a chilled cocktail glass. Garnish with the lemon peel, and serve.

peking-style caramelized walnuts

THE ONLY TRICK TO MAKING THESE FABULOUS SUGAR-COATED WALNUTS IS TO PLAN AHEAD TO HAVE ENOUGH TIME to let them dry and cool. Believe me, it's worth it.

Makes 2 cups

2 cups whole shelled walnuts

½ cup granulated sugar

2 cups corn or peanut oil

1 tablespoon sesame seeds

Bring a large pot of water to a boil. Add the walnuts, and simmer for 5 minutes. Drain in a colander. Do not rinse.

Pat the warm walnuts dry, and transfer to a large bowl. Sprinkle with the sugar, and gently toss to coat completely. Spread the walnuts out in a single layer on a rimmed baking sheet, and let them dry at room temperature overnight.

Heat the oil in a deep skillet or Dutch oven. When the oil is just beginning to bubble, fry the walnuts, gently stirring with a slotted spoon, until the sugar melts and the walnuts turn golden, 3 to 5 minutes. Remove with the spoon, and transfer to a wire rack set over a foil-lined baking sheet. Sprinkle with the sesame seeds, and let cool completely. The walnuts will keep in an airtight jar for up to 2 weeks.

roasted edamame

HERE IS A BAR SNACK THAT IS VERY EASY TO PREPARE. WHEN EDAMAME ARE ROASTED THEY TAKE ON A DELICIOUS nutty flavor. A few bowls of these are perfect nibbles to add to your cocktail buffet table.

Makes about 2 cups

16 ounces frozen shelled edamame, thawed and drained

2 tablespoons olive oil

¼ teaspoon Chinese five-spice powder

Kosher salt and freshly ground black pepper

Fresh lemon juice, for serving

Preheat the oven to 375°F.

Line a baking sheet with paper towels and arrange the edamame on them in a single layer. Pat the edamame dry and transfer to a large bowl. Add the olive oil, five-spice powder, and generous amounts of salt and pepper to the bowl and toss until coated.

Spread the edamame on a baking sheet in a single layer and roast for 30 to 35 minutes, turning occasionally, until they are browned and begin to pop.

Let the edamame cool for about 5 minutes, sprinkle them with lemon juice, and serve at once.

sriracha deviled eggs

SRIRACHA SAUCE IS A SPICY BLEND OF RED JALAPEÑOS WITH PLENTY OF GARLIC, VINEGAR, SUGAR, AND SALT, and I always have a large bottle of it in my refrigerator. This addictively pungent sauce adds a layer of heat and flavor to all kinds of dishes, like soups, noodles, burgers, and sandwiches, to name just a few. When sriracha is added to plain deviled eggs, they are transformed into a taste sensation.

Makes 12 deviled eggs

6 large eggs

½ cup mayonnaise

1 teaspoon Dijon mustard

2 teaspoons sweet pickle relish

1 teaspoon sriracha

Kosher salt and freshly ground black pepper

Put the eggs in a large saucepan, and add cold water to cover. Bring to a gentle boil over medium-high heat. When the water just begins to boil, remove the pot from the heat, and cover tightly. Let the eggs stand, covered, for 10 minutes. Drain the eggs, and rinse them under cold running water. Pat the eggs dry, and let them cool completely.

When the eggs are cool enough to handle, peel them, and cut them in half lengthwise. Gently scoop the yolks into a large bowl, being careful not to break the whites. Arrange the egg white halves on a platter, cavity-side up, and set aside.

Mash the egg yolks with a fork; stir in the mayonnaise, mustard, relish, and sriracha sauce, and mix well. Season to taste with salt and pepper.

Using a small spoon, mound the filling in the cavities of the egg white halves, dividing it evenly. The deviled eggs may be refrigerated for up to 3 hours before serving. Serve chilled or at room temperature.

tuna tartare on toasted wontons

THE FRESH, CLEAN FLAVORS OF TUNA, LIME, AND OLIVE OIL BLEND BEAUTIFULLY WITH SESAME-TOASTED WONTONS. Tuna tartare is a snap to make—just be sure to use "sushi-quality" tuna, which is the freshest and best you can buy. Chop it on a clean work surface with a sharp knife, toss it with the other ingredients, and let it marinate for up to two hours—any longer, and it will become mushy. This recipe also works very well with sushi-quality salmon. These wontons are wonderful little treats to serve with sake drinks or martinis.

Serves 8

1 pound sushi-quality fresh tuna

2 tablespoons finely chopped fresh cilantro

2 tablespoons finely chopped fresh flat-leaf parsley

1 tablespoon minced shallot

1 teaspoon finely grated fresh ginger

2 teaspoons olive oil

Salt and freshly ground black pepper

Sesame oil for brushing

16 wonton wrappers (see Note)

2 teaspoons fresh lime juice

6 scallions (white and green parts), trimmed and minced, for garnish

Sesame seeds, for garnish

Using a sharp knife, dice the tuna as finely as possible. Transfer to a medium bowl, and add the cilantro, parsley, shallot, ginger, olive oil, and salt and pepper to taste. Gently mix until the ingredients are thoroughly combined. Cover, and refrigerate for 1½ to 2 hours.

Preheat the oven to 350°F. Brush a baking sheet with sesame oil.

Cut the wonton wrappers diagonally in half to make triangles. Place them on the baking sheet, and lightly brush them with a bit more sesame oil. Bake until just lightly browned and crisp, 4 to 5 minutes. Remove from the oven, and set aside to cool a bit.

When ready to serve, gently toss the lime juice with the tuna. Spoon the tuna tartare onto the wontons, garnish with scallions and sesame seeds, and serve at once.

Note: Wonton wrappers are available at Asian markets, health food stores, and gourmet supermarkets.

lemon-poached shrimp
with sriracha-lime mayonnaise

THESE SHRIMP CAN BE SERVED WITH OR WITHOUT THEIR SHELLS, BUT I PREFER TO SERVE THEM PEEL-AND-EAT style. The shells are loaded with flavors from fresh lemon and herbs and Old Bay seasoning.

Serves 6

1 teaspoon kosher salt

2 lemons, halved

3 bay leaves

3 sprigs fresh thyme

3 sprigs fresh flat-leaf parsley

¼ cup Old Bay seasoning

2 pounds jumbo or extra-large shrimp, unpeeled

Sriracha-Lime Mayonnaise (recipe follows), for serving

Lime wedges, for serving

Fill a large pot with water. Add the salt, squeeze the lemon juice into the water, and add the lemon halves. Add the bay leaves, thyme and parsley sprigs, and Old Bay. Bring to a boil over medium-high heat, and simmer for 10 minutes.

Reduce the heat to medium and add the shrimp. Simmer, uncovered, until the shrimp turn bright pink and their tails curl. Remove from the poaching liquid with a slotted spoon. Do not rinse. Chill the shrimp thoroughly.

Serve the shrimp, peeled or unpeeled, with the Sriracha Mayonnaise and lime wedges.

sriracha-lime mayonnaise

Makes about ½ cup

½ cup mayonnaise

2 tablespoons fresh lime juice

1 teaspoon sriracha sauce

Kosher salt and freshly ground
   black pepper

Put the mayonnaise in a mixing bowl. Add the lime juice and sriracha sauce and mix together. Add salt and pepper to taste, and chill before serving. The mayonnaise will keep in the refrigerator, covered, for 2 days.

teriyaki chicken wings

WHETHER THEY'RE GRILLED OR PREPARED IN THE OVEN, THESE TANGY, TASTY WINGS MAKE A FABULOUS SNACK
to have with drinks. You just may want to double the recipe.

Serves 6

½ cup soy sauce

¼ cup orange juice

2 tablespoons vegetable oil

2 tablespoons sake or dry sherry

2 tablespoons plain rice vinegar

1 tablespoon honey

2 teaspoons grated fresh ginger

2 garlic cloves, thinly sliced

3 pounds whole chicken wings

**6 scallions (white and green parts),
  minced, for garnish**

**2 tablespoons sesame seeds,
  for garnish**

Combine the soy sauce, orange juice, oil, sake, vinegar, honey, ginger, and garlic in a blender, and blend until smooth.

Put the chicken wings in a large nonreactive bowl, and pour the marinade over them. Cover, and marinate in the refrigerator for at least 4 hours or overnight.

To broil the chicken wings: Preheat the broiler. Arrange the chicken pieces and half of the marinade in a shallow pan. Broil about 6 inches from the heat for about 8 minutes; turn and baste the chicken, and broil for another 8 to 10 minutes until golden brown.

To grill the chicken wings: Prepare a gas or charcoal grill. Remove the wings from the marinade, and grill them over medium-low heat, turning once, until golden brown, about 15 minutes.

Heat the remaining marinade in a saucepan over high heat to bring to a boil. Reduce the heat to medium and maintain a simmer for 3 minutes. Arrange the chicken wings on a platter, garnish with the scallions and sesame seeds, and serve at once with the remaining marinade as a dipping sauce.

pork katsu & pickled cucumber bites

PORK KATSU, WHICH IS SIMPLY A BREADED AND FRIED PORK CUTLET, IS A VERY POPULAR JAPANESE DISH. MY variation of katsu is to cut these crispy treats into bite-size pieces and serve them with pickled cucumbers and a scallion-soy dipping sauce. These Asian bites are terrific with sake drinks (page 92 and 94) or gimlets (page 95).

Serves 4 to 6

½ cup all-purpose flour

2 eggs, lightly beaten

1 tablespoon Worcestershire sauce

1½ cups panko bread crumbs

6 thin, boneless pork cutlets
   (about 1¼ pounds)

Peanut, corn, or vegetable oil,
   for frying

Pickled Cucumbers (recipe follows)

Scallion-Soy Sauce (recipe follows),
   for serving

Wasabi mustard, for serving
   (optional)

Put the flour in a shallow bowl. Put the eggs in a second shallow bowl, and whisk in the Worcestershire sauce. Put the panko crumbs in a third shallow bowl.

Dip each cutlet in the flour (shake off the excess); dip in the egg mixture (shake off the excess); and dredge in the panko crumbs, making sure that each cutlet is covered.

Heat a large skillet over medium-high heat, pour in ¼ inch of oil, and heat until very hot but not smoking. Put the cutlets in the pan; shake and tilt the pan so the oil rolls over the pork, and cook until the cutlets are golden on the bottom, about 3 minutes. Flip them, shaking and tilting the pan again, and cook until the other side is golden, 2 to 3 minutes. Transfer the pork to a plate lined with paper towels. Repeat with the remaining cutlets.

Cut the cutlets into bite-size pieces, top each piece with a cucumber round, and serve with toothpicks. Serve with the Scallion-Soy Sauce and mustard, if using.

pickled cucumbers

Makes about 2 dozen

**8 ounces Kirby cucumbers,
   sliced into thin rounds**

1 teaspoon kosher salt

1 teaspoon sugar

Put the cucumbers in a bowl. Toss them together with the salt and sugar. Set aside for at least 30 minutes before using.

scallion-soy sauce

Makes about ¾ cup

½ cup soy sauce

2 tablespoons rice wine vinegar

1 teaspoon toasted sesame oil

**2 scallions (white and green parts),
   minced**

In a small bowl, whisk together the soy sauce, vinegar, sesame oil, and scallions. Set aside until ready to serve.

korean short rib tacos

KOREAN SHORT RIBS, CALLED KALBI OR GALBI, ARE A MAINSTAY OF KOREAN COOKING. TRY THESE SLOW-COOKED ribs with warm corn tacos, pungent Sesame-Lime Sauce, and Pickled Red Onions—they can all be made well in advance—for a delicious Asian-style happy hour. The onions should be in everyone's recipe repertoire. They are simple to make and add extra zesty flavor to all kinds of dishes, such as tacos, sandwiches, salads, and sautéed vegetables.

Serves 6

3 pounds bone-in beef short ribs

Kosher salt and freshly ground black pepper

3 tablespoons vegetable oil

1 yellow onion, chopped

¼ cup soy sauce

¼ cup mirin

2 tablespoons sake

2 (1-inch) pieces fresh ginger, peeled and thinly sliced

2 whole star anise

12 small corn tortillas

Sesame-Lime Sauce (recipe follows), for serving

Pickled Red Onions (recipe follows), for serving

Season the ribs generously with salt and pepper. Heat the oil in a large stockpot or Dutch oven over medium-high heat. When it starts to shimmer, add the short ribs in a single layer, being careful not to crowd the pan, and working in batches if necessary. Sear until deeply browned on all sides, about 4 minutes per side. Transfer the ribs to a platter. Pour off and reserve all but 1 tablespoon of the fat from the pot.

Add the onion, and cook over medium heat until softened and golden, about 5 minutes. Add 1 cup of water, the soy sauce, mirin, sake, ginger, and star anise. Return the ribs to the pot, and bring the mixture to a boil. Decrease the heat to low, cover, and cook at a bare simmer for 2½ to 3 hours, stirring and turning the ribs occasionally, until the meat is very tender.

Lift the cooked short ribs out of the braising liquid and transfer them to a bowl. When cool enough to handle, shred the meat, discard the bones, and set aside.

Preheat the oven to 200°F. Warm the tortillas by wrapping them in aluminum foil and heating in the oven for at least 20 minutes.

Strain the braising liquid, and discard the solids. (To defat the sauce, refrigerate it for an hour or two, until the fat congeals on the top; scrape it off and discard.) Pour the sauce back into the pot over medium-high heat, and cook the sauce, uncovered, until it is very syrupy and reduced to about 1 cup, 10 to 15 minutes. Add the shredded meat to the sauce, and mix well. Keep warm at a slow simmer.

sesame-lime sauce

Makes about ¼ cup

Juice of 1 lime

**½ teaspoon sambal oelek
  (Asian garlic-chili sauce)**

3 tablespoons sesame oil

Whisk together, and set aside until ready to serve.

pickled red onions

Makes about 2 cups

½ cup white vinegar

3 tablespoons granulated sugar

Pinch of kosher salt

1 teaspoon mustard seeds

1 teaspoon whole black peppercorns

**1 small dried chile or
  a pinch of red pepper flakes**

**1 large red onion, peeled and
  cut into thin rings**

In a small nonreactive saucepan, bring the vinegar and sugar to a boil, stirring until the sugar dissolves. Add the salt, mustard seeds, peppercorns, and chile; lower the heat, and simmer, stirring, for 1 minute. Add the onion, and simmer for 1 more minute. Remove from the heat, and let cool completely. Transfer the onions and liquid to a glass jar. Cover tightly, and chill in the refrigerator for at least 2 hours before serving. The onions will keep in the refrigerator, covered, for up to 2 weeks.

grilled beef & asparagus yakitori with peanut-ginger dipping sauce

SAVORY GRILLED BEEF, ASPARAGUS, AND SCALLIONS ON SKEWERS ARE GREAT STARTERS FOR A SUMMER DINNER party. I like to use the double-skewer method because they make handling skewers on the grill much easier. The 2 skewers should be parallel with approximately ½ inch between them. Serve them with deliciously smooth Peanut-Ginger Dipping Sauce.

Makes 12 skewers

⅓ cup soy sauce

⅓ cup rice wine vinegar

1 tablespoon fish sauce (*nam pla*)

1 teaspoon sesame oil

1 teaspoon sriracha sauce

1 tablespoon minced fresh ginger

1 tablespoon packed brown sugar

1 pound beef tenderloin,
    cut into 1-inch pieces

8 ounces fresh asparagus, trimmed

12 scallions (white and green parts),
    trimmed and cut into 2-inch pieces

Peanut-Ginger Dipping Sauce
    (recipe follows), for serving

Soak 24 long bamboo skewers in water for 30 minutes.

In a large nonreactive bowl, whisk together the soy sauce, vinegar, fish sauce, sesame oil, sriracha sauce, ginger, and brown sugar until combined. Transfer half of the marinade to a small bowl, and set aside. Add the beef to the larger bowl, toss to coat, and let stand for 30 minutes.

Meanwhile, bring a medium saucepan of water to a boil, add the asparagus, and cook until just tender, about 3 minutes. Drain the asparagus, rinse, and let cool.

Thread 2 pieces each of the asparagus, beef, and scallions on 2 parallel skewers. (Each piece of meat or vegetable will have two skewers going through it.) Cover, and chill the skewers until ready to grill.

Prepare a gas or charcoal grill. Grill the skewers over medium-high heat, for 2 to 3 minutes per side, for medium-rare. Serve with Peanut-Ginger Dipping Sauce.

peanut-ginger dipping sauce

Makes about ½ cup

2 tablespoons smooth peanut butter

2 tablespoons plain yogurt

2 tablespoons soy sauce

1 tablespoon fresh lime juice

1 tablespoon peeled and finely chopped fresh ginger

½ teaspoon toasted sesame oil

Dash of hot sauce

Combine the peanut butter, yogurt, soy sauce, lime juice, ginger, sesame oil, and hot sauce in a blender; blend until very smooth. Taste, and adjust the seasonings as necessary. The sauce will keep in the refrigerator, covered, for up to 2 days. Bring to room temperature before serving.

asian influences

::::::::::::

COCKTAILS

cucumber & basil martini

COOL CUCUMBER AND SAVORY BASIL ARE SENSATIONAL ADDITIONS TO A DRY MARTINI. THIS IS A GOOD DRINK to accompany a seafood bite, such Tuna Tartare on Toasted Wontons (page 78) or Lemon-Poached Shrimp (page 81).

Serves 1

¼ **cup peeled and chopped cucumber, plus a thin slice for garnish**

3 **basil leaves, divided**

2 **ounces gin or vodka**

1½ **ounces dry vermouth**

Muddle the chopped cucumber and two of the basil leaves in the bottom of a cocktail shaker. Fill the shaker with ice, and add the gin and vermouth. Shake well, and strain into a chilled martini glass. Garnish with the cucumber slice and the remaining basil, and serve.

sake dry martini

BECAUSE OF ITS CLEAN, FRESH FLAVOR AND LOW ALCOHOL CONTENT, SAKE IS AN EXCELLENT MIXER IN COCKTAILS. Try it as a substitute for vermouth in a martini.

Serves 1

3 **ounces vodka or gin**

½ **ounce sake**

1 **lemon slice, for garnish**

Fill a cocktail shaker with ice, and add the gin or vodka and sake. Shake well, and strain into a chilled martini glass. Garnish with the lemon slice, and serve.

Cucumber & Basil Martini

sake & ginger cocktail

THIS REFRESHING BOURBON DRINK IS MADE WITH FRESH ORANGE JUICE AND FRESHLY GRATED GINGER AND is finished with a splash of ginger beer. It pairs well with many spicy, soy sauce–based Asian dishes.

Serves 1

2 ounces bourbon

¾ ounce sake

½ ounce fresh orange juice

Dash of simple syrup (page 13)

1 teaspoon grated fresh ginger

Splash ginger beer

Orange peel, for garnish

Fill a cocktail shaker with ice, and add the bourbon, sake, orange juice, simple syrup, and ginger. Shake well, and strain into a tall glass filled with ice. Add a splash of ginger beer. Garnish with the orange peel, and serve.

haiku cocktail

I LOVE THIS LIGHT COCKTAIL. IT'S MEANINGFUL, SHORT, AND TO THE POINT, LIKE HAIKU.

Serves 1

2 ounces sake

Dash of dry vermouth

1 thin cucumber slice, for garnish

Fill a cocktail shaker with ice; add the sake and vermouth. Shake well, and strain into a chilled martini glass. Garnish with the cucumber slice, and serve.

ginger-lime gimlet

THIS IS A TART AND REFRESHING COCKTAIL THAT GOES WELL WITH A NUMBER OF ASIAN SNACKS. DO NOT EVEN think about using lime juice from a bottle—only freshly squeezed will do.

Serves 1

3 ounces vodka or gin

2 ounces fresh lime juice

2 ounces ginger syrup (page 15)

1 lime wedge, for garnish

Fill a cocktail shaker with ice, and add the vodka, lime juice, and ginger syrup. Shake well, and strain into a chilled martini glass. Garnish with the lime wedge, and serve.

singapore sling

THE SINGAPORE SLING HAS A LONG AND STORIED HISTORY, AND THE ONLY FACT THAT COCKTAIL HISTORIANS CAN agree on is that the drink was created by Mr. Ngiam Tong Boon for the Raffles Hotel in Singapore around 1913. After that, the origin stories diverge. But I think all will agree that this is a mighty tasty cocktail.

Serves 1

1½ ounces gin

½ ounce Cherry Heering or cherry brandy

¼ ounce Cointreau

¼ ounce Benedictine

2 ounces pineapple juice

½ ounce fresh lime juice

Dash of Angostura bitters

Splash of club soda

1 orange slice, for garnish

1 Marinated Fresh Cherry (page 12) or maraschino cherry, for garnish

Fill a cocktail shaker with ice, and add the gin, Cherry Heering, Cointreau, Benedictine, pineapple juice, lime juice, and bitters. Shake well, and strain into a highball glass filled with ice. Top with a splash of club soda. Garnish with the orange slice and cherry, and serve.

kimchi bloody mary

THIS UTTERLY DELICIOUS BLOODY MARY VARIATION COMES FROM THE BAR AT DOKEBI, A SMASHING KOREAN restaurant in Brooklyn that serves wonderful food and drinks. The restaurant makes its own kimchi, but it is also available in Asian markets, in the refrigerator section of many supermarkets, and online.

Serves 6

1 (46-ounce) bottle tomato
 or vegetable juice

1 ounce fresh lemon juice

1 ounce fresh lime juice

2 tablespoons prepared horseradish

1 tablespoon Worcestershire sauce

Dash of Tabasco or hot sauce

1 tablespoon green olive juice

2 tablespoons kimchi juice

Freshly ground black pepper

12 ounces vodka

Kimchi, green olives, lemon wedges,
 lime wedges, and celery sticks
 for garnish

To prepare the Bloody Mary mix, combine the tomato juice, lemon juice, lime juice, horseradish, Worcestershire sauce, Tabasco sauce, olive juice, kimchi juice, and black pepper to taste in a large container with a tight-fitting lid. Cover tightly, and shake vigorously. The Bloody Mary mix may be made up to 2 days ahead. Chill in the refrigerator.

Fill each glass with ice cubes, add 2 ounces of vodka, top off with the Bloody Mary mix, and stir. Add a generous spoonful of kimchi to each glass, and stir again. Garnish each drink with olives, lemon and lime wedges, and a celery stick. For extra spiciness, add additional Tabasco sauce and pepper.

watermelon cosmo

WHAT COULD BE MORE SUMMERY AND REFRESHING THAN A DRINK MADE WITH FRESH, CHILLED WATERMELON JUICE? Just toss chunks of ripe watermelon in a blender, and blend until smooth. You may want to strain the juice, but I prefer it a little chunky.

Serves 1

1½ ounces vodka

1 ounce triple sec

½ ounce fresh lime juice

2 ounces chilled watermelon juice (see Note)

6 fresh mint leaves

1 lime slice, for garnish

Fill a cocktail shaker with ice, and add the vodka, triple sec, lime juice, watermelon juice, and mint. Shake well, and strain into a martini glass. Garnish with the lime slice, and serve.

Note: To make the watermelon juice, slice the watermelon in half, remove the seeds, and scoop chunks of the flesh in a blender. Discard the rind. Blend the watermelon until it is totally pulverized, about 1 minute. Add the juice of 1 lime, and blend for a few seconds. Strain the juice, if desired, transfer it to a pitcher, and chill for at least 2 hours. Stir the juice with a long spoon if necessary.

CHAPTER 5
latin flavors

spicy roasted garbanzos

GARBANZO BEANS, OR CHICKPEAS, ARE VERSATILE, HEALTHY, AND DELICIOUS, AND IT'S ALWAYS A GOOD IDEA
to have a few cans of them on hand. Here's an easy recipe that blends them with a bit of olive oil and some hot
and smoky spices before roasting them into a perfect, crunchy cocktail party snack.

Makes 2 cups

2 (15-ounce) cans garbanzo beans, rinsed and drained

2 tablespoons olive oil

1 teaspoon ground cumin

1 teaspoon hot smoked paprika

Pinch of cayenne pepper

Kosher salt

Lime wedges, for serving (optional)

Preheat the oven to 400°F. Line a baking sheet with parchment paper.

Put the garbanzo beans on a clean kitchen towel or paper towels, gently rub them dry, and let them sit on the towel to dry out for 15 to 20 minutes.

In a medium bowl, mix together the olive oil, cumin, paprika, and cayenne pepper. Add the garbanzo beans, and toss well to coat. Arrange the beans in a single layer on a baking sheet. Sprinkle generously with salt. Bake, shaking the pan occasionally, until golden and crispy, 25 to 30 minutes. Let them cool a bit, and transfer to a bowl. Sprinkle with more salt, if necessary, and serve with lime wedges, if desired.

tomatillo salsa

TOMATILLOS, OR *TOMATOES VERDE*, ARE AN IMPORTANT STAPLE IN MEXICAN COOKING, AND TOMATILLO SALSA IS A savory complement to any number of dishes—tacos, grilled meat and fish, eggs. This is an excellent accompaniment to Corn & Cheese Arepas (page105) and Grilled Spicy Steak & Pepper Kebabs (page 113). Tomatillos have the same growing season as tomatoes and are available at many supermarkets, farmers' markets, and Mexican grocery stores.

Makes about 2 cups

1 pound tomatillos, husked, rinsed and halved or quartered, depending on size

1 white onion, peeled and quartered

2 garlic cloves, thinly sliced

1 large jalapeño pepper, seeded and minced (see Note)

½ cup chopped fresh cilantro

2 tablespoons fresh lime juice

Kosher salt and freshly ground black pepper

Fill a medium saucepan with 1 inch of water. Add the tomatillos, onion, and jalapeños, bring to a boil, and simmer over medium heat until they are slightly soft, about 5 minutes. Drain, and reserve the cooking liquid. Set aside, and let cool.

Transfer the cooked tomatillos to a blender, and blend until smooth. Add a bit of the reserved liquid to thin to your desired consistency. Add the cilantro, lime juice, and salt and pepper to taste, and blend again. Taste, and adjust the seasonings as necessary. Serve chilled or at room temperature.

Note: If you prefer a hotter salsa, do not seed the jalapeño pepper. Be sure to wash your hands thoroughly after handling the pepper.

corn & cheese arepas

I LIKE TO MAKE THESE PANCAKE-LIKE AREPAS IN SUMMER WHEN SWEET CORN IS SEASON AND IN ABUNDANCE AT farm stands and markets. These wonderful bite-sized nibbles, garnished with salsa, pickled onions, and hot sauce, go well margaritas (pages 116 and 117), Spicy Tequila Bloody Marys (page 120) and Micheladas (page 119).

Serves 6 to 8

1 cup cornmeal

Pinch of sugar

1 egg

1 cup whole milk

1 cup shredded cheddar cheese (about 4 ounces)

½ cup cooked corn kernels (from 1 ear of fresh corn)

Corn or canola oil, for cooking

Tomatillo salsa (page 103), pickled onions (page 87), hot sauce, and sour cream, for garnish

In a large bowl, combine the cornmeal and sugar. In another bowl, whisk together the egg, milk, cheese, and corn and fold into the cornmeal mixture until well blended.

Heat the oil in a large skillet over medium heat. When it begins to shimmer, spoon tablespoons of the batter into the pan, and cook until the bottoms are golden brown, about 2 minutes. Flip the arepas, and cook until the other sides are golden brown, about 2 minutes. Drain on paper towels.

If not serving right away, put the arepas in a baking dish and keep in a warm oven (200°F) until ready to serve. Serve with tomatillo salsa, pickled onions, hot sauce, and sour cream.

chicken & cheese quesadillas
with avocado cream

THESE SCRUMPTIOUS QUESADILLAS TASTE GREAT WITH MARGARITAS (PAGE 116 AND 117) OR SPICY TEQUILA
Bloody Marys (page 120). You can also make them with shredded turkey or duck. The silky-smooth avocado cream
is a fabulous addition to quesadillas. And it could become your go-to sauce to drizzle over soups, salads, and eggs,
as well.

Serves 6

8 (7½-inch to 8-inch)
   flour tortillas

1 cup (about 4 ounces) shredded
   Monterey Jack cheese, divided

1 cup (about 4 ounces)
   crumbled soft goat cheese, divided

1 cup shredded cooked chicken

4 white mushrooms, stemmed
   and thinly sliced

3 scallions (white and green parts),
   thinly sliced

2 tablespoons chopped fresh cilantro

Avocado Cream (recipe follows),
   for drizzling

Lime wedges, for serving

Hot sauce, for serving

Preheat the oven to 250°F. Put 4 tortillas on a work surface, Sprinkle half of the Monterey Jack and goat cheeses evenly over the tortillas.

Scatter the chicken evenly over the cheeses, and sprinkle the mushrooms, scallions, and cilantro over the chicken. Cover evenly with the remaining cheeses. Put the second tortilla over each, and press down with a spatula.

Heat a dry nonstick skillet over medium heat until very hot. Put a quesadilla in the skillet, and cook, pressing down with the spatula for about 3 minutes, until lightly browned on the bottom. Turn the quesadilla, and cook until the bottom is browned and the cheese is melted, about 3 minutes. Transfer to a baking sheet, and keep warm in the oven. Repeat with the remaining quesadillas.

To serve, drizzle each quesadilla with the avocado cream, cut into sixths, and serve hot with lime wedges and hot sauce.

avocado cream

Makes 1 cup

1 ripe avocado, halved, pitted, peeled, and cut into small pieces

2 tablespoons fresh lime juice

2 tablespoons light sour cream or crème fraîche

Kosher salt

Hot sauce (optional)

In the bowl of a food processor, combine the avocado, lime juice, sour cream, salt to taste, and hot sauce, if using. Pulse until very smooth and serve at once.

wild mushroom & cheese quesadillas

THESE QUESADILLAS ARE A PERFECT DISH FOR VEGETARIANS. THEY'RE FULL OF THE WOODSY FLAVOR OF WILD mushrooms and warm, melted cheese. To serve these, set out bowls of salsa, pickled onions, sour cream, and sriracha sauce for your guests to use as garnishes. This recipe can be easily doubled to feed a crowd.

Serves 6

3 tablespoons olive oil

3 shallots, peeled and finely chopped

1 cup chopped wild mushrooms (about 1 pound) such as cremini, shiitake, porcini, and Portobello

1 teaspoon chili powder

Kosher salt and freshly ground black pepper

8 (7½-inch to 8-inch) flour tortillas

1 cup (about 4 ounces) shredded Monterey Jack cheese

1 cup (about 4 ounces) crumbled soft goat cheese

Salsa, pickled onions (page 87), sour cream, sriracha sauce, chopped fresh cilantro, and lime wedges, for garnishes

Preheat the oven to 250°F.

Heat the olive oil in a large skillet over medium heat. Add the shallots, and cook until softened, about 5 minutes. Add the mushrooms, and cook, stirring occasionally, until they begin to soften and brown, about 5 minutes. Add the chili powder and season to taste with salt and pepper, and cook, stirring occasionally, for 3 more minutes. (Note: The mushrooms can be prepared a few hours ahead of time. Cover, and set aside. Reheat before proceeding.)

Put 4 tortillas on a work surface. Sprinkle the Monterey Jack, the mushroom mixture, and the goat cheese evenly over the tortillas. Put the second tortilla over each, and press down with a spatula.

Heat a dry nonstick skillet over medium heat until very hot. Put a quesadilla in the skillet, and cook, pressing down with the spatula for about 3 minutes until lightly browned on the bottom. Turn the quesadilla, and cook until the bottom is browned and the cheese is melted, about 3 minutes. Transfer to a baking sheet, and keep warm in the oven. Repeat with the remaining quesadillas.

To serve, cut each quesadilla into sixths, and serve with desired condiments.

chicken, chorizo & avocado tacos

HERE'S A TASTY RECIPE THAT MAKES GOOD USE OF LEFTOVER CHICKEN. WHEN PREPARING THIS FILLING, BE SURE TO cook the onions and peppers very slowly over low heat so they soften and caramelize before you add the chorizo and chicken. These tacos can be topped with Oaxaca cheese (a semi-soft cow's milk cheese), mozzarella, or goat cheese.

Makes 8 tacos

2 tablespoons corn oil

1 red onion, thinly sliced

1 red bell pepper, stemmed, seeded, and cut into 2-inch strips

Kosher salt and freshly ground black pepper

4 ounces chorizo, diced

2 cups cooked shredded chicken

8 (6-inch) flour or corn tortillas

1 avocado, halved, pitted, peeled, and diced

½ cup crumbled Oaxaca, mozzarella, or goat cheese

½ cup chopped fresh cilantro

Lime wedges, salsa, and hot sauce for serving

Heat the oil in a large skillet over medium heat. Add the onion, reduce the heat to low, and cook for 15 minutes. Add the red pepper, season to taste with salt and pepper, and continue to cook, stirring occasionally, until softened and caramelized, 15 to 20 minutes.

Add the chorizo, and cook, stirring occasionally, for 15 minutes. Add the chicken, and cook for 10 minutes.

Preheat the oven to 350°F. Put the tortillas on a baking sheet, and heat until warmed through, about 5 minutes. Transfer the tortillas to a large platter.

Spoon the chicken mixture in the center of each tortilla, top with avocado, and sprinkle with cheese and cilantro. Serve with lime wedges, salsa, and hot sauce.

black bean & spinach tacos

TACOS ARE GREAT TO SERVE TO A CROWD, AND THESE DELICIOUS ONES THAT ARE MADE WITH BLACK BEANS AND spinach will please vegetarians and meat eaters alike. You can assemble them yourself or, better yet, put all of the garnishes out, and have your guests customize their own tacos.

Makes 12 tacos

3 tablespoons olive oil, divided

1 red onion, finely diced

2 garlic cloves, minced

1 red bell pepper, stemmed, seeded and finely diced

2 jalapeño peppers, stemmed, seeded, and finely diced

1 teaspoon cumin

1 teaspoon chili powder

2 (15-ounce) cans black beans, rinsed and drained

1 cup chopped fresh or canned tomatoes, with their juice

Kosher salt and freshly ground black pepper

2 packed cups chopped fresh spinach (about 4 ounces)

12 (6-inch) flour or corn tortillas

½ cup shredded Monterey Jack cheese (about 2 ounces)

Sliced avocados, chopped fresh tomatoes, chopped fresh cilantro, lime wedges, and hot sauce, for garnish

Heat 2 tablespoons of the olive oil in a large skillet over medium heat. Add the onion, garlic, red pepper, and jalapeño peppers, and cook until softened, about 5 minutes. Add the cumin and chili powder, and cook, stirring occasionally, for 3 minutes.

Add the beans and tomatoes, season to taste with salt and pepper, and cook over medium heat, stirring occasionally, until the liquid is absorbed, about 15 minutes.

Meanwhile, heat the remaining tablespoon of oil in a sauté pan. Add the spinach, and sauté until just wilted, about 3 minutes. Set aside. (The beans and spinach can be cooked a few hours ahead of time.) Add the spinach to the beans, and cook, stirring, until combined.

Preheat the oven to 350°F. Put the tortillas on baking sheets, and heat until warmed through, about 5 minutes. Transfer the tortillas to a large platter.

Top each tortilla with the bean mixture. Garnish with cheese, avocados, tomatoes, and cilantro, and serve with lime wedges and hot sauce.

grilled spicy steak & pepper kebabs with lemon-paprika aioli

THIS IS A GOOD GRILLED SNACK-ON-A-STICK TO SERVE WITH CAIPIRINHAS (PAGE 123) OR PISCO SOURS (PAGE 118) at a backyard barbecue. These skewers can also be made in the broiler for an indoor party.

Makes 12 skewers

Juice of 1 lime

2 tablespoons olive oil

2 garlic cloves, thinly sliced

1 teaspoon cumin

1 teaspoon chili powder

½ jalapeño pepper, seeded
   and chopped

Kosher salt and freshly ground
   black pepper

1 pound flank steak

3 red bell peppers, stemmed, seeded,
   and cut into 24 (1-inch) pieces

6 to 8 scallions, (white and light
   green parts), cut into 1-inch pieces

Lemon-Paprika Aioli
   (recipe follows)

Soak 12 wooden skewers in water for 30 minutes to an hour.

In a small bowl, whisk together the lime juice, olive oil, garlic, cumin, chili powder, jalapeño, and salt and pepper to taste. Put the flank steak in a nonreactive baking dish, pour the marinade over top, and turn the meat to coat evenly. Let the meat marinate at room temperature for 1 hour or in the refrigerator for up to 4 hours.

Remove the meat from the marinade, and cut it into 24 (1-inch) cubes. Thread each skewer with a piece of scallion, bell pepper, meat, bell pepper, meat, and end with a piece of scallion.

Prepare a gas or charcoal grill. Grill the skewers over medium-high heat, turning occasionally, 8 to 10 minutes for medium-rare. To prepare the skewers in the oven: Heat the broiler. Put the skewers on a broiler pan about 5 to 6 inches from the heat. Broil for 4 to 5 minutes, turn, and broil for about 5 minutes longer for medium-rare. Serve at once with Lemon-Paprika Aioli.

lemon-paprika aioli

Makes about 1¼ cups

2 egg yolks

1 garlic clove, finely minced

2 tablespoons fresh lemon juice

1 cup corn oil

1 teaspoon smoked paprika

Pinch cayenne pepper

**Kosher salt and freshly ground
  black pepper**

In a medium bowl, whisk together the egg yolks, garlic, and lemon juice. Gradually add the oil in a thin stream, whisking constantly, until thickened. Whisk in the paprika, cayenne pepper, and salt and pepper to taste. The sauce will keep in the refrigerator, covered, for up to 2 days.

latin flavors

::::::::::::

COCKTAILS

classic margarita on the rocks

THE BALANCE OF SWEET, SALTY, AND TART FLAVORS IN A MARGARITA MAKES IT A VERY POPULAR AND FOOD-FRIENDLY cocktail. Really, what goes better with salty tortilla chips and guacamole or spicy salsa? You can serve margaritas in so many ways: with or without salt, in a blender with ice to make them frozen, or shaken with a different-flavored liqueur.

Serves 1

Kosher salt, for rimming the glass

1 lime wedge, for rimming the glass

2 ounces tequila

1 ounce Cointreau

¾ ounce fresh lime juice

1 lime slice, for garnish

Pour the salt onto a small, shallow plate. Rub the outside rim of a cocktail glass or coupe with the lime wedge. Dip it into the plate of salt to coat the rim of the glass.

Fill a cocktail shaker with ice, and add the tequila, Cointreau, and lime juice. Shake well, and strain into the prepared glass. Garnish with the lime slice, and serve.

grand margarita

FOR A CHANGE OF PACE TRY A MARGARITA MADE WITH GRAND MARNIER INSTEAD OF COINTREAU. IT INFUSES THE drink with a delicious and intense orange flavor.

Serves 1

Kosher salt, for rimming the glass

1 lime wedge, for rimming the glass

2 ounces tequila

1 ounce Grand Marnier

¾ ounce fresh lime juice

1 orange slice, for garnish

Pour the salt onto a small, shallow plate. Rub the outside rim of a cocktail glass or coupe with the lime wedge. Dip it into the plate of salt to coat the rim of the glass.

Fill a cocktail shaker with ice, and add the tequila, Grand Marnier, and lime juice. Shake well, and strain into the prepared glass. Garnish with the orange slice, and serve.

frozen margarita

FROZEN MARGARITAS ARE A HAPPY HOUR FAVORITE, AND HERE IS A RECIPE FOR A BIG TASTY PITCHERFUL TO WHIP UP in the blender. It's a good idea to use an electric citrus juicer when juicing the limes for these drinks.

Serves 6

Kosher salt, for rimming the glasses

1 lime wedge, for rimming the glasses

1½ cups crushed ice

12 ounces tequila

8 ounces Cointreau

6 ounces fresh lime juice

6 lime slices, for garnish

Pour the salt onto a small, shallow plate. Rub the outside rim of 6 cocktail glasses or coupes with the lime wedges. Dip them into the plate of salt to coat the rims of the glasses.

Put the crushed ice in a blender. Add the tequila, Cointreau, and lime juice, and blend until smooth. Pour into the prepared glasses, garnish with the lime slices, and serve.

la paloma

IF YOU WANT TO SERVE A DRINK LIKE A LOCAL IN MEXICO, PREPARE A PALOMA INSTEAD OF A MARGARITA, WHICH IS usually made with inexpensive grapefruit soda. It is also terrific with freshly squeezed grapefruit juice. It's sweet, sour, salty, and refreshing—all you can ask for in a drink.

Serves 1

2 ounces tequila

Juice of ½ lime

Pinch of salt

3 ounces fresh grapefruit juice

3 ounces club soda

1 lime wedge, for garnish

Put the tequila, lime juice, and salt in a highball glass. Add ice, top with grapefruit juice and soda, and stir gently. Garnish with the lime wedge, and serve.

pisco sour

PISCO, THE NATIONAL SPIRIT OF PERU, IS A BRANDY THAT IS DISTILLED FROM SEVERAL DIFFERENT VARIETIES OF grapes grown in South America. This drink has a nice bite to it.

Serves 1

1½ ounces Pisco

¾ ounce fresh lime juice

½ ounce simple syrup (page 13)

1 small egg white

2 dashes Angostura bitters

1 lime wedge, for garnish

Fill a cocktail shaker with ice. Add the Pisco, lime juice, simple syrup, and egg white. Shake well, and strain into a small cocktail glass. Splash in the bitters and garnish with the lime wedge.

michelada

THIS POPULAR BEER COCKTAIL ORIGINALLY CAME FROM MEXICO CITY. I FIRST TASTED ONE AT ROBERTO SANTIBAÑEZ'S fabulous restaurant, Fonda, on Manhattan's Lower East Side. Here is my version of this tasty refresher and, I might add, hangover cure.

Serves 1

Kosher salt, for rimming the glass

1 lime wedge, for rimming the glass

1 ounce fresh lime juice

½ teaspoon Worcestershire sauce

**⅛ teaspoon freshly ground
black pepper**

4 dashes Tabasco or Cholula Sauce

**1 (12-ounce) bottle of Mexican beer,
such as Tecate or Dos Equis**

Pour the salt onto a small, shallow plate. Rub the outside rim of a pint glass with the lime wedge. Dip it into the plate of salt to coat the rim of the glass.

Add the lime juice, Worcestershire sauce, pepper, and Tabasco to the glass. Fill the glass with ice and beer.

spicy tequila bloody mary

THE FLAVOR COMBINATION OF TEQUILA, TOMATOES, AND SMOKED PAPRIKA IN THIS DRINK IS WONDERFUL. SERVE these with quesadillas (pages 106 and 108) and lots of toppings. ¡Qué divertido!

Serves 6

1 (46-ounce) bottle tomato
 or vegetable juice

1 ounce fresh lemon juice

1 tablespoon Tabasco sauce
 or Louisiana hot sauce

2 tablespoons prepared horseradish

1 tablespoon Worcestershire sauce

Pinch celery salt

Freshly ground black pepper

Pinch smoked paprika

Pinch red pepper flakes

1 ounce fresh lime juice

12 ounces tequila

Lime wedges and cherry tomatoes,
 for garnish

Combine the tomato juice, lemon juice, Tabasco sauce, horseradish, Worcestershire sauce, celery salt, and black pepper to taste in a large container with a tight-fitting lid. Cover tightly, and shake vigorously. The Bloody Mary mix may be made up to 3 days ahead. Chill in the refrigerator.

Add the paprika, red pepper flakes, and lime juice to the Bloody Mary mix, and stir well. Fill each glass with ice cubes, add 2 ounces of tequila, top off with the Bloody Mary mix, and stir. Garnish with a lime wedge and a cherry tomato, and serve.

caipirinha

THIS BRAZILIAN DRINK IS MADE WITH CACHAÇA, FRESH LIMES, AND SUGAR. CACHAÇA IS A LIQUOR THAT IS DISTILLED from sugarcane juice, and its taste is similar to tequila.

Serves 1

½ **lime, cut into 4 wedges**

1 teaspoon sugar

2 ounces cachaça

Put the lime wedges and sugar in a rocks glass. Muddle the lime and sugar together to extract as much juice as possible. Add the cachaça and stir. Fill the glass with ice, stir again, and serve.

CHAPTER 6

island fever

island crab spread

THIS DELIGHTFUL CRABMEAT SPREAD GETS ITS UNIQUE FLAVOR FROM JAMAICAN PICKAPEPPA SAUCE. SERVE it on buttered toast points or crackers, or stuff it into endive leaves for a great-tasting and great-looking appetizer.

Makes about 1 cup

**4 ounces cream cheese,
    at room temperature**

2 tablespoons sour cream

1 tablespoon fresh lemon juice

½ tablespoon horseradish

1 tablespoon chili sauce

1 teaspoon Pickapeppa Sauce

½ teaspoon sweet smoked paprika

2 tablespoons chopped red onion

**8 ounces lump crabmeat,
    pick over and drained**

**Kosher salt and freshly ground
    black pepper**

**Buttered toast points, crackers,
    or endive leaves, for serving**

Put the cream cheese, sour cream, lemon juice, horseradish, chili sauce, Pickapeppa Sauce, paprika, and red onion in a food processor, and blend until smooth. Transfer the mixture to a bowl.

Fold in the crabmeat, and add salt and pepper to taste. Cover, and chill for at least 4 hours before serving.

caribbean pan-seared shrimp with lime

THIS HERB-INFUSED SHRIMP IS A DISH TYPICAL OF THE FRENCH CARIBBEAN. THE SHRIMP MARINATES FOR A BIT IN garlic, oil, and fresh herbs and is then quickly seared in a dry skillet. Serve this satisfying hors d'oeuvre (or main dish) with lots of lime, hot sauce, and a beachy drink like Planter's Punch (page 146) or a Flamingo Cocktail (page 143).

Serves 4

1 pound large shrimp, peeled and deveined, tails left on

2 tablespoons olive oil

1 tablespoon minced garlic

1 tablespoon chopped fresh rosemary leaves

1 tablespoon chopped fresh thyme

Pinch of cayenne pepper

Kosher salt and freshly ground black pepper

Lime wedges, for serving

Hot sauce, for serving

Combine the shrimp, olive oil, garlic, rosemary, thyme, cayenne pepper, and salt and pepper to taste in a large nonreactive bowl, and let the shrimp marinate at room temperature for 1 hour.

Heat a dry nonstick skillet over medium heat until hot. Add the shrimp, and cook, stirring, until they turn bright pink and are cooked through, 6 to 8 minutes.

Serve at once with lime wedges and hot sauce.

shrimp & avocado ceviche

CEVICHE IS USUALLY MADE WITH RAW FISH THAT IS "COOKED" IN A MARINADE OF LIME OR OTHER CITRUS JUICE. If you want to make ceviche with shrimp or another shellfish, keep in mind that it should be lightly poached before it is added to the marinade. This lively shrimp ceviche is splendid way to kick off the evening.

Serves 6

½ cup plus 2 tablespoons
   fresh lime juice
   (from about 4 limes), divided

1 pound small shrimp

½ red onion, finely chopped

2 tablespoons ketchup

2 tablespoons chili sauce

Dash of hot sauce

1 cup peeled and diced cucumber

1 small ripe avocado, halved,
   pitted, peeled, and cut
   into small dice

⅓ cup fresh cilantro

Kosher salt and freshly ground
   black pepper

Lime wedges, for garnish

Tortilla chips or crackers,
   for serving

Bring a large pot of salted water to a boil, and add 2 tablespoons of the lime juice. Add the shrimp, bring to a boil, and cook until just pink, 2 to 3 minutes. Drain, and rinse under cold water. Drain again, and peel and devein the shrimp. Toss with the remaining ½ cup of lime juice in a nonreactive container, cover, and refrigerate for 1 hour.

Remove the shrimp with a slotted spoon to a large nonreactive bowl, and reserve the lime juice. Add the onion, ketchup, chili sauce, hot sauce, cucumber, avocado, and cilantro, and mix gently. Add a few spoonfuls of the reserved lime juice to your desired taste. Season with salt and pepper to taste and toss again. Serve at once, or let the ceviche chill in the refrigerator for up to 2 hours. Garnish with lime wedges, and serve with tortilla chips or crackers and additional hot sauce.

cod & crabmeat fritters

TASTY, LIGHT FRITTERS MADE WITH POACHED COD AND CANNED CRABMEAT MAKE A GOOD AND CRUNCHY BITE TO serve with any number of island-style drinks. Other white fish such as halibut, hake, or flounder may be used instead of cod.

Serves 4 to 6

½ **pound cod fillets**

½ **white onion, roughly chopped**

1 **celery rib, roughly chopped**

1 **carrot, roughly chopped**

1 **sprig parsley**

½ **cup all-purpose flour**

½ **cup chickpea flour**

Pinch cayenne pepper

Kosher salt and freshly ground black pepper

1 **egg, light beaten**

2 **scallions (white and green parts), finely minced**

1 **jalapeño pepper, stemmed, seeded, and finely minced**

2 **tablespoons finely chopped fresh cilantro**

1 **cup lump crabmeat, picked over**

Canola oil, for frying

Fresh lime wedges, for serving

Hot sauce, for serving

In a pan large enough to poach the fish in, combine the fish, onion, celery, carrot, and parsley. Cover with water, bring to a boil and reduce the heat so the water is barely simmering. Simmer for 6 minutes. Drain and let cool. Flake the fish with a fork and set aside.

In a large bowl, whisk together the all-purpose flour, chickpea flour, cayenne pepper, and salt and pepper to taste. Stir in the egg and 1 cup of water and mix together. Add the scallions, jalapeño, cilantro, the fish and crabmeat and stir well. The batter can be stored covered in the refrigerator for up to 3 hours.

Pour the oil to a depth of ¼ inch into a large skillet and heat until smoking. Drop the batter by teaspoonful into the oil. Fry until just golden underneath, about 2 minutes. Turn and fry the other side until crisp and golden, about 3 minutes. Drain on paper towels and serve at once with lime wedges and hot sauce.

pan-seared scallops

HERE IS A QUICK AND EASY PREPARATION OF SAUTÉED FRESH SCALLOPS AND JERK SEASONING THAT IS FINISHED with spritzes of fresh lemon and lime. Look for Jamaican jerk seasoning (not the paste or sauce form) in the spice section of the supermarket or online. These are quite delicious on their own, but you can also serve the scallops with spicy Remoulade Sauce (page 27) or Sriracha-Lime Mayonnaise (page 82).

Serves 4 to 6

12 sea scallops (about 1 pound)

**Kosher salt and freshly ground
black pepper**

1 tablespoon jerk seasoning

2 tablespoons olive oil

1 tablespoon fresh lemon juice

1 tablespoon fresh lime juice

**1 tablespoon finely chopped
fresh flat-leaf parsley**

**1 tablespoon finely chopped
fresh cilantro**

Pat the scallops dry and cut them in half. Sprinkle generously with salt and pepper to taste and jerk seasoning.

Heat the oil in a large nonstick skillet over medium heat until hot but not smoking. Add the scallops and sear until golden brown, about 3 minutes per side.

Remove the scallops from the heat to a platter and sprinkle with the lemon and lime juice and the parsley and cilantro. Serve at once with toothpicks.

fish tacos with citrus slaw

I LIKE TO USE TILAPIA FILETS FOR MAKING FISH TACOS BECAUSE THE FLAVORS OF CHILI POWDER, CUMIN, AND fresh lime blend beautifully with the fish. These are great to serve with zesty citrus slaw and extra toppings like fresh tomatoes, scallions, and avocados.

Serves 8

½ teaspoon chili powder

½ teaspoon cumin

¼ teaspoon cayenne pepper

¼ teaspoon sweet paprika

2 tablespoons olive oil, divided

Juice of 1 lime

Kosher salt and freshly
  ground black pepper

2 (6-ounce) tilapia fillets

Corn oil, for frying

8 (6-inch) tortillas

Citrus Slaw (recipe follows),
  for serving

½ cup sour cream or crema,
  for serving

Chopped tomatoes, for serving

Chopped scallions, for serving

Diced avocados, for serving

Hot sauce, for serving

Lime wedges, for serving

In a small bowl, mix together the chili powder, cumin, cayenne, 1 tablespoon of the olive oil, and the lime juice. Arrange the fish in a nonreactive dish, brush both sides with the spice mixture, and season with to taste with salt and pepper. Let the fish marinate at room temperature for 20 to 30 minutes.

Heat a large nonstick skillet or grill pan over medium heat. Brush the pan with the remaining tablespoon of olive oil, and sauté or grill the fish until lightly browned and cooked through, about 4 minutes per side.

Transfer the fish to an ovenproof dish, and break the fish into bite-sized pieces. If not serving right away, cover with foil, and keep warm in a 200°F oven.

Heat 1 teaspoon of corn oil in a large skillet over medium-high heat. Cook the tortillas until lightly browned, about 30 seconds per side, adding more oil as necessary. Drain the tortillas on paper towels.

Divide the fish among the tortillas, and top with the Citrus Slaw. Serve with the sour cream, additional toppings, lime, and hot sauce.

citrus slaw

Serves 8

**2 cups finely shredded
green cabbage**

½ cup thinly sliced red onion

2 carrots, peeled and shredded

¼ cup chopped fresh cilantro

3 tablespoons olive oil

2 tablespoons fresh lime juice

2 tablespoons fresh orange juice

Pinch of sugar

**Kosher salt and freshly ground
black pepper**

Combine the cabbage, onion, carrot, and cilantro in a large bowl. In a small bowl, whisk together the olive oil, lime juice, sugar, and salt and pepper to taste. Pour the marinade over the cabbage mixture, and toss together. Let the slaw marinate for 1 hour or up to 8.

cubanos

IF YOU'RE CONSIDERING MAKING A PORK ROAST FOR DINNER, PREPARE A SLOW-COOKED CUBAN PORK ROAST and use the delicious leftovers to make Cubanos. These warm, crispy, and sumptuous sandwiches are really fun to make and serve with a few rounds of mojitos (page 141). If you do not have a Cuban sandwich press (plancha), you can press the top of the sandwich with a heavy object such as a skillet or even a foil-wrapped brick. Aficionados say that an authentic Cubano has no tomato, no lettuce, and no mayo. Ever.

Serves 6 to 8

1 loaf Cuban bread or 4 (6-inch) hero rolls (see Note)

3 tablespoons unsalted butter, at room temperature

Yellow mustard

12 to 16 slices dill pickles

1 pound Cuban Pork Roast (recipe follows)

½ pound ham, thinly sliced

½ pound Swiss cheese sliced

Cooking spray or butter

Cut the bread in half lengthwise and cut into quarters. (If using hero rolls, just cut them lengthwise.) Spread the butter on the cut sides each of piece of bread. Spread the mustard on one half of the bread. Layer with pickles, pork, ham, and cheese.

Heat a heavy skillet or grill pan over medium-high heat. Coat the pan with cooking spray or melted butter. Put the sandwiches in the pan. Press the sandwiches down with a plancha, or a heavy object such as a skillet, and cook for 3 minutes, Turn the sandwiches and repeat until the cheese is melted and the bread is golden brown, 3 to 5 minutes. Slice each sandwich in half diagonally and serve.

Note: Cuban bread can be found at Latin bakeries, some supermarkets, and online.

slow-cooked cuban roast pork

Serves 6 to 8

½ cup fresh orange juice

½ cup fresh lime juice

1 tablespoon ground oregano

1 teaspoon cumin

Kosher salt and freshly
  ground black pepper

1 large red onion, sliced

2 garlic cloves, thinly sliced

One 5- to 6-pound pork shoulder

In a small bowl, whisk together the orange juice, lime juice, oregano, cumin, and salt and pepper to taste. Add the onion and garlic and whisk again. Put the pork and the marinade in a large zip-top plastic bag or a nonreactive dish. Cover and refrigerate overnight.

Preheat the oven to 275°F. Bring the pork and marinade to room temperature and transfer them to a large Dutch oven or roasting pan with a lid. Cover and roast until very tender, turning occasionally, at least 5 hours.

Let the pork cool a bit, then slice it and serve with the juices.

grilled jamaican jerk chicken wings

THESE SMOKY, FIERY JERK WINGS NEED A BIT OF TIME TO PREPARE—A DAY TO MARINATE AND A SHORT BAKE IN THE oven before grilling. Plan accordingly, because they are so worth it. Serve with Gin & Ginger Beers (page 145) and lots of napkins.

Serves 6

1 jalapeño, serrano, or Scotch bonnet
  pepper, seeded and minced

2 scallions (white and green parts),
  trimmed and minced

1 onion, chopped

2 garlic cloves, chopped

1 tablespoon grated fresh ginger

1 teaspoon chopped fresh thyme

1 teaspoon allspice

2 tablespoons vegetable oil

2 tablespoons soy sauce

3 tablespoons fresh lime juice

2 tablespoons packed brown sugar

Kosher salt and freshly ground
  black pepper

12 whole chicken wings
  (about 2½ pounds)

Lime wedges, for serving

Hot sauce, for serving

The day before serving, combine the pepper, scallions, onion, garlic, ginger, thyme, allspice, oil, soy sauce, lime juice, brown sugar, ½ cup water, and salt and pepper in a blender, and blend until fairly smooth.

Using a sharp knife or kitchen shears, separate the chicken wings at the joint. Pour the marinade into a large, shallow dish, add all the chicken pieces, and turn to coat. Cover, and refrigerate overnight. Bring to room temperature before proceeding.

Prepare a charcoal or gas grill. Preheat the oven to 400°F. Bake the chicken wings for 15 minutes, turn and baste the wings, and bake for an additional 15 minutes. Transfer the wings to the grill, and cook over medium heat, turning occasionally, until well-browned and cooked through, 10 to 15 minutes. Transfer the chicken to a platter, and serve with lime wedges and hot sauce.

island fever

:::::::::::

COCKTAILS

Mojito

mojito

A COOL AND QUENCHING MOJITO IS A BEAUTIFUL THING. AND WHILE THERE ARE MANY VARIATIONS OF THIS DRINK that originated in Cuba, its traditional ingredients are mint, rum, simple syrup, fresh lime juice, and club soda.

Serves 1

4 fresh mint sprigs, divided

1 ounce simple syrup (page 13)

1 ounce fresh lime juice

2 ounces white rum

Club soda or seltzer

Put 2 mint sprigs, the simple syrup, and the lime juice in a highball glass, and muddle together. Fill the glass with ice, add the rum, and stir to blend. Fill the glass with club soda, garnish with the remaining mint sprigs, and serve.

passionfruit mojito

HERE IS A LOVELY VERSION OF THE TRADITIONAL MOJITO THAT ADDS DARK RUM AND PASSIONFRUIT TO THE MIX. Passionfruit juice is available in the international and refrigerated sections of the market.

Serves 1

4 fresh mint sprigs, divided

1 ounce simple syrup (page 13)

1 ounce fresh lime juice

2 ounces dark rum

2 ounces passionfruit juice

Club soda or seltzer

Put 2 mint sprigs, the simple syrup, and the lime juice in a highball glass, and muddle together. Fill the glass with ice, add the rum and the passionfruit juice, and stir to blend. Fill the glass with club soda, garnish with the remaining mint sprigs, and serve.

daiquiri

THE CLASSIC DAIQUIRI, NAMED AFTER THE CUBAN TOWN WHERE IT WAS INVENTED, IS NOTHING LIKE THE SWEET, blended fruit drinks that share the name. This refreshing drink is made with rum, fresh lime juice, and a bit of simple syrup. That's it.

Serves 1

1½ ounces light rum

1 ounce simple syrup (page 13)

¾ ounce fresh lime juice

1 lime slice, for garnish

Fill a cocktail shaker with ice. Add the rum, simple syrup, and lime juice, and shake well. Strain into a cocktail glass. Garnish with the lime slice, and serve.

cuba libre

THIS IS A SUBLIMELY SIMPLE DRINK—RUM, COKE, AND LIME. SOME PEOPLE PREFER TO MAKE THIS WITH DARK, stronger-flavored rum, but it's entirely up to you.

Serves 1

Juice of ½ fresh lime

2 ounces white rum

4 ounces Coca Cola

1 lime slice, for garnish

Pour the lime juice into a highball glass. Fill the glass with ice, pour in the rum and soda, and stir well. Garnish with the lime slice, and serve.

flamingo cocktail

THE FLAMINGO IS A VERSION OF A CUBA LIBRE (OPPOSITE PAGE) THAT USES GRAPEFRUIT SODA INSTEAD OF COKE. this recipe comes from Jim Meehan, the renowned mixologist at PDT bar in New York. It's a nice, refreshing drink that goes well with spicy food.

Serves 1

2 ounces white rum

¾ ounce fresh lime juice

3 ounces pink grapefruit soda

1 lime slice, for garnish

Fill a cocktail shaker with ice. Add the rum and lime juice, and shake well until chilled. Strain into a rocks glass, and add the soda. Garnish with the lime slice, and serve.

Dark & Stormy

dark & stormy

AN AUTHENTIC DARK & STORMY IS MADE WITH VERY DARK RUM, SUCH AS GOSLING'S BLACK SEAL FROM BERMUDA.

Serves 1

1 lime wedge

½ teaspoon granulated sugar

2 ounces dark rum

4 ounces ginger beer

Put the lime wedge and sugar in a highball glass, and muddle together. Add the rum, and stir. Fill the glass with ice, top with ginger beer, and serve.

gin & ginger beer

SPARKLING GINGER BEER ADDS A NICE HERBAL FLAVOR TO THIS COOLING DRINK. BE SURE TO ADD IT TO YOUR summer party menu.

Serves 1

2 ounces gin

1 teaspoon granulated sugar

Juice of ½ lemon

Ginger beer

1 orange slice, for garnish

Mint leaves, for garnish

Fill a cocktail shaker with ice. Add the gin, sugar, and lemon juice, and shake well. Strain into a tall glass. Add ice, and top off with ginger beer. Stir gently. Garnish with the orange slice and mint leaves, and serve.

salty dog

THIS TART AND REFRESHING DRINK SHOULD BE MADE WITH FRESHLY SQUEEZED GRAPEFRUIT JUICE, AND ALTHOUGH it is traditionally made with vodka, gin works well, too.

Serves 1

Kosher salt

1 strip grapefruit peel

2 ounces vodka or gin

5 ounces grapefruit juice, preferably fresh-squeezed

Pour the salt onto a small, shallow plate. Rub the outside rim of a cocktail glass with the grapefruit peel. Dip the glass into the plate of salt to coat the rim.

Fill the glass with ice, add the vodka and grapefruit juice, and stir.

planter's punch

DEPENDING ON WHOM YOU ASK, THIS OUTSTANDING WARM-WEATHER PUNCH COMES FROM EITHER JAMAICA, Barbados, Martinique, or the Planter's Hotel in St. Louis. No matter where it comes from, it is refreshing, cooling, and downright delicious—perfect for slow sipping on a summer evening.

Serves 6

6 ounces dark rum

6 ounces light rum

3 ounces triple sec

12 ounces orange juice, preferably fresh-squeezed

12 ounces pineapple juice

3 ounces fresh lime juice

1 ounce Grenadine syrup

1 teaspoon Angostura bitters

6 orange slices, for garnish

Fill a large pitcher with ice, and add the rums, triple sec, orange juice, pineapple juice, lime juice, Grenadine, and bitters. Stir well, until the pitcher is frosty. Fill 6 highball glasses with ice, and strain the punch into the glasses. Garnish each drink with an orange slice, and serve.

zombie punch

HERE IS A TERRIFIC TROPICAL PUNCH RECIPE THAT IS SURE TO LIVEN UP YOUR HAPPY HOUR. IT'S FUN TO WHIP UP an icy pitcher or two of these fresh and fruity drinks just before your guests arrive, so you won't be tending bar for most of the party.

Serves 6

6 ounces dark rum

6 ounces light rum

6 ounces apricot brandy

10 ounces orange juice, preferably fresh-squeezed

4 ounces fresh lemon juice

4 ounces fresh lime juice

2 ounces Grenadine syrup

½ teaspoon Angostura bitters

6 pineapple wedges or orange wedges, for garnish

Fresh mint leaves, for garnish

Fill a large pitcher with ice, and add the rums, brandy, orange juice, lemon juice, lime juice, Grenadine, and bitters. Stir well, until the pitcher is frosty. Fill 6 highball glasses with crushed ice, and strain the punch into the glasses. Garnish each drink with a pineapple or orange slice and mint leaves, and serve.

acknowledgments

My thanks and gratitude go out to the people who worked with me on this book:

Rita Maas, for her wonderful food photography, as always.

Adrienne Anderson, for her brilliant food styling, bar tending, and for exhibiting great grace under pressure.

Mariellen Melker for her lovely prop styling and to Scarlett Alley in Philadelphia, Pennsylvania and Crate & Barrel in King of Prussia, Pennsylvania for the use of their goods for styling.

Natalia del Rivero, Designer, for the use of her beautiful apartment for location shooting.

Angela Miller, my agent, who made this book happen.

The people at Running Press, especially Kristen Green Wiewora, who helped me develop so many ideas for this book with her smart and insightful suggestions, and to Frances Soo Ping Chow for her creative support.

The many chefs and bartenders who generously shared their food and drinks recipes, tips, and secrets with me.

My family, Lester, Zan, and Isabelle, for always being there for me and for everything else.

index